D0796255

# The Definitive Guide to Shopify Themes

## Master the Design Skills to Build World-Class Ecommerce Sites

**Gavin Ballard**

Apress®

*The Definitive Guide to Shopify Themes*

Gavin Ballard
Melbourne, Victoria, Australia

ISBN-13 (pbk): 978-1-4842-2640-7          ISBN-13 (electronic): 978-1-4842-2641-4

DOI 10.1007/978-1-4842-2641-4

Library of Congress Control Number: 2017952538

Cover image designed by Freepik

Managing Director: Welmoed Spahr
Editorial Director: Todd Green
Acquisitions Editor: Louise Corrigan
Development Editor: James Markham
Technical Reviewer: Keir Whitaker
Coordinating Editor: Nancy Chen
Copy Editor: Kezia Endsley
Compositor: SPi Global
Indexer: SPi Global
Artist: SPi Global

Distributed to the book trade worldwide by Springer Science+Business Media New York, 233 Spring Street, 6th Floor, New York, NY 10013. Phone 1-800-SPRINGER, fax (201) 348-4505, e-mail orders-ny@springer-sbm.com, or visit www.springeronline.com. Apress Media, LLC is a California LLC and the sole member (owner) is Springer Science + Business Media Finance Inc (SSBM Finance Inc). SSBM Finance Inc is a **Delaware** corporation.

For information on translations, please e-mail rights@apress.com, or visit http://www.apress.com/rights-permissions.

Apress titles may be purchased in bulk for academic, corporate, or promotional use. eBook versions and licenses are also available for most titles. For more information, reference our Print and eBook Bulk Sales web page at http://www.apress.com/bulk-sales.

Any source code or other supplementary material referenced by the author in this book is available to readers on GitHub via the book's product page, located at www.apress.com/9781484226407. For more detailed information, please visit http://www.apress.com/source-code.

Printed on acid-free paper

*To my family and friends, within and without the world of Shopify.*

# Table of Contents

# About the Author

 **Gavin Ballard** has been tinkering with all things Shopify for nearly a decade. While working on a couple of small projects (including his own side business selling posters), he became fascinated with the platform and the potential it had to transform online commerce.

He started to share what he was learning through his blog and forum posts and to build tools to help other theme developers get the most out of the platform. However, it wasn't until a client reached out to him on the strength of his "Bootstrap for Shopify" project that he fell into Shopify freelancing full-time.

In 2015, Gavin founded **Disco**, a Shopify Plus Partner studio based in Melbourne, Australia. Specializing in the development of custom applications, Disco works with some of the largest Shopify merchants around the world to push the limits of what's possible with the platform and to deliver solutions to help merchants take their businesses to the next level.

Gavin is now recognized as one of the leading Shopify Experts in the world, and he continues to share his Shopify knowledge through writing, in-person workshops and meetups, contributions to open source projects, and courses and books such as this one.

As he is always happy to shoot the breeze and chat Shopify, you can follow Gavin on Twitter (@gavinballard) or reach out directly via e-mail (gavin@gavinballard.com).

# About the Technical Reviewer

**Keir Whitaker** has been making a living with web technologies since 2000 and has held a variety of positions for both agencies and corporate organizations. Additionally, he's worked as a freelance web developer, technical consultant, and event curator.

Since 2012, he has been working at Shopify, helping grow the Partner Program and building a community around designers and frontend developers using the platform.

As well as his work at Shopify, he also occasionally gets behind the microphone to record an episode of the web industry focused podcast *The Back to Front Show* (backtofrontshow.com). You can find out more about Keir on his web site (keirwhitaker.com) or connect to him on Twitter (@keirwhitaker) and by e-mail (hello@keirwhitaker.com).

# Acknowledgments

As I will rave to any and all who care to listen, Shopify's "secret sauce" doesn't lie in its code but in its ecosystem—the employees, experts, and partners who work together to "make commerce better for everyone." It's a cheesy sentiment but genuine—I would never have been able to write this book or do the work I enjoy without help from the people listed here.

To the many Shopifolk and Shopify Partners I've crossed paths with over the years, thank you for your time and generosity—whether answering forum posts, helping with blog articles, diving in to obscure Liquid problems, or collaborating on new and exciting projects. There are too many of you to mention, but a special shout-out to Carson Shold, Jason Bowman, Courtney Symons, and Rhys Furner from Shopify, and Jessica Claesson, Galen King, Stewart Knapman, Mack Johnson, Chris Pointer, Kurt Elster, Justin Metros, Rick Davies, Dave Lazar, Cal Wilson, Alex O'Byrne, and Piers Thorogood from the Partner community for help with an earlier version of the book (and general Shopify awesomeness).

Special thanks need to go to Scott Hay at One Inch Round for being the best first client one could ask for; Louise Corrigan and Nancy Chen at Apress for their patience and persistence in getting the book over the line; and of course the inimitable Keir Whitaker at Shopify.

Finally, my eternal gratitude to my colleagues at Disco, my family, and my friends for their support.

# Introduction

Back in 2005, Shopify got off the ground when a couple of folks in Canada wanted to sell snowboards online but couldn't find an Ecommerce platform to meet their needs.

Since then, the capabilities of the Shopify, the number of merchants using it, and the world of Ecommerce in general has come a long way. At the time of writing, the platform powers the online stores of over 500,000 businesses across 175 countries, with 2,500 of those being high-volume merchants on the newer "enterprise" offering, Shopify Plus. A total of $15.4 billion in transactions was processed by Shopify in 2016, a doubling of the previous year's total.

Many point to Shopify's hosted nature, its expanding range of features, or its partnerships with major companies like Facebook, Twitter, and Amazon as core to its success. In my opinion, one of the most critical and oft-overlooked factors underlying Shopify's growth is its ecosystem of Partners—a broad spectrum of developers, designers, marketers, and experts who work with Shopify merchants to help them grow and succeed on the platform. Being one of these Partners myself, I guess this opinion comes off as quite self-serving, but I feel that anyone who's worked with Shopify in any capacity would have to acknowledge that at the very least, the Partner ecosystem is a major asset.

Partners are the ones helping merchants transition to Shopify, building out their stores, customizing their themes, and configuring the multitude of available applications. They're also the ones developing themes and apps for sale in Shopify's official Stores, making a living and building businesses on top of the platform.

I first came to Shopify as a tinkerer quite early in its history, in 2008. The feature set was limited; APIs were undocumented and the default themes merchants could choose from when setting up your store weren't going to win any design awards. Getting things to work was often a matter of trial, error, and swearing at Liquid code. Still, it was streets ahead of any other platform at the time in terms of ease-of-use, and there was something about the way the company seemed dedicated to improve that made it interesting enough to stick around (Tobi, then and now Shopify's CEO, would often be in the Partner forums responding to issues directly with a "just rolling out some code to fix that now!").

Sticking around has proven to be a good decision—in 2013 I could make the transition to full-time Shopify freelance work; in 2015 I founded Disco, a studio that helps Shopify merchants grow and improve their businesses. Over that time, I've worked on stores large and small, built themes and applications from scratch, written and released open-sourced libraries, and partnered with Shopify to deliver talks, workshops, and online courses. Most importantly, I've had the chance to meet scores of amazing Partners and "Shopifolk," discover the world of Ecommerce through the eyes of merchants, and make friends with a diverse range of people from across the world.

This book is an attempt to share some of the things this experience has taught me.

# Why This Book?

No one resource can equip a person with every specific thing they need to know about Shopify themes. There are too many edge cases, too many wonderful quirks in the world of online commerce, for a one-stop shop to deliver on that promise.

Fortunately, for the Shopify developer faced with learning the ropes or tackling a new requirement, there's already quite a wealth of information at hand. Shopify's official Theme and Liquid documentation is professional and thorough, and they often publish detailed "How-to" guides on the official Partner Blog. Shopify Partners themselves often fill in the gaps with blog posts and code examples, and for those still struggling to find answers, there are healthy communities of folk willing to help on the official Shopify forums or in unofficial Slack groups.

So why add one more voice to the mix?

Despite that breadth of information already out there, I've long felt there's something missing—something that allows a novice Shopify theme developer to tie all these disparate bits of of knowledge together into a single narrative. In this book, I'm trying to fill this gap by covering both high-level theme design principles *and* practical coding skills, and using case studies and examples wherever possible to tie the two together.

The goal here isn't to replicate existing documentation or to provide a step-by-step rote-learning approach for every conceivable scenario you'll face as a theme developer. Rather, by reading this book, you should acquire a deeper understanding of how Shopify themes work, how you can rely upon fundamental principles of theme design when faced with new situations, and how you can level up the workflow processes you use to deliver a professional final product.

# Who This Book Is For

This book assumes that you have a working knowledge of the fundamentals of web design and development—HTML, CSS, and JavaScript. It does **not** assume any prior knowledge of Shopify development (we'll kick things off with a Shopify primer in Chapter 1).

Developers with some Shopify experience may find some of the earlier material straightforward, but will derive value from the coverage of topics such as workflow automation, development best practices, and deeper dives into the architecture and design principles of Shopify themes.

Veteran Shopify developers are likely to get something out of the material as well—whether it's an introduction to advanced theme deployment techniques, taking performance optimization to a new level, or simply getting a different perspective on theme development.

# Structure of This Book

This book is broken into 11 chapters. Each one tackles a different idea or component of Shopify theme development, and while their contents are somewhat independent, they do follow an overall chronological order. This is especially true for Chapters 4 through 7, which together walk through the process of building an entire Shopify theme from scratch.

I would therefore recommend working through the book in order the first time around, and then coming back to specific chapters and sections as needed for reference.

Throughout the book, I use code snippets to demonstrate concepts and specific techniques. For space reasons, many of these listings are truncated to show only the more important parts—the full versions of these are available in the resources repository on GitHub, located at `https://github.com/Apress/definitive-guide-to-shopify-themes`. A second GitHub repository, `https://github.com/gavinballard/defguide-theme`, tracks the full source code development for the example theme begun in the exercises in Chapter 4 and built on in the remaining chapter exercises.

# Beyond the Book

As I mentioned, there are several places to go to find help if you find yourself stuck or want to learn more about a topic. Outside of the standard Google search, you can search through the official Shopify forums (`https://ecommerce.shopify.com/forums`), check out the official theme documentation (`https://help.shopify.com/themes`), or browse through posts on the Partner Blog (`https://www.shopify.com/partners/blog`).

There's also a growing number of Shopify-focused communities being built on a range of social platforms, including Slack, Reddit, and Facebook.

If you have any specific questions about the material in this book, or you would like to report errata, you can contact me directly at `gavin@gavinballard.com`.

On with the show!

# CHAPTER 1

# A Shopify Theme Primer

For some content platforms, the word "theme" means a limited degree of control. It evokes the idea of selecting from a few predefined choices, perhaps picking a color scheme or replacing some images.

Shopify themes are more than that; they give storeowners complete control over every aspect of the frontend of their sites, including HTML, stylesheets, and scripts. This, I believe, is one of Shopify's greatest strengths. It's why it can be suitable for solo entrepreneurs starting their first business while at the same time supporting Fortune 500 companies.

This chapter starts by explaining how Shopify gives us that flexibility. It covers the directory structure of a theme package, explains Liquid (Shopify's templating language) a little better, explains how assets are handled, and gives us a sense of how these parts work together to deliver a usable shopping experience to our customers.

## Anatomy of a Shopify Theme

One Shopify store can have many themes installed, although only one can be published and visible to the public at any given time. Themes can come from different sources—purchased from the official Shopify Theme Store (`https://themes.shopify.com`), downloaded from a third-party marketplace, built for a specific customer by a freelancer or agency, or developed in-house by the merchant.

Each theme installed into a Shopify store is presented in the Online Store - Themes section of the Shopify Admin, as shown in Figure 1-1.

© Gavin Ballard 2017
G. Ballard, *The Definitive Guide to Shopify Themes*, DOI 10.1007/978-1-4842-2641-4_1

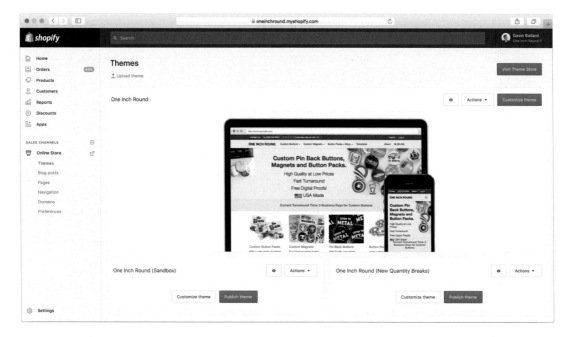

***Figure 1-1.*** *The Themes List in the Shopify Admin. Note that one theme (the large one at the top) is "published," meaning it's currently active and being displayed to customers. The other themes are installed but only visible to the storeowner in a "preview" mode*

New themes can be added to a Shopify store in two ways: directly from the Theme Store, or by uploading a .zip file containing files in the standard theme directory structure. Themes can then be "previewed" prior to publishing, giving the store owner the chance to see how a new theme will look and feel before pushing it out to real customers.

When a customer visits a page on the storefront, Shopify looks at the files contained in a theme to find the appropriate template files to render and uses them in combination with "dynamic" information (such as the store's current inventory, details of the logged-in customer, and the contents of the cart) to generate HTML, which is then delivered to the browser. In this way, Shopify themes operate in a similar fashion to many template-based platforms or programming languages used to generate dynamic, content-driven web sites, such as WordPress or Drupal.

# Theme Structure

Regardless of their source, all Shopify themes share a common format under the hood: a package of files arranged in a specific directory structure, as shown in Figure 1-2.

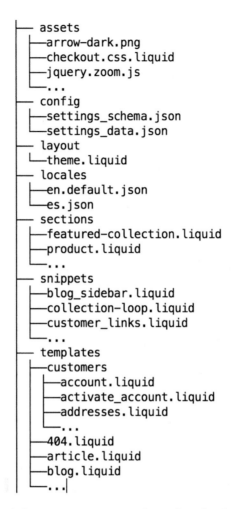

**Figure 1-2.** *The standard directory structure for a finished Shopify theme*

As you can see, the structure is quite flat, with seven top-level directories (and one subdirectory) containing a large number of Liquid template files (.liquid), configuration files (.json), and assets (.css, .js, .png, etc.).

*Assets* include all the static assets you'd like to use with your theme, like images, stylesheets, and scripts. Shopify has built-in support for Sass stylesheets (with some limitations, discussed shortly), so if you're a Sass aficionado, you can simply save files with a .scss extension directly in your theme. Your theme's assets are automatically served from Shopify's CDN.

*Config* is a directory containing specifications for global theme settings, which allow theme designers to create themes that give merchants control and flexibility over the layout, appearance, and data model of their storefront. Theme settings are presented to store owners with the markup defined in `settings_schema.json` and, when saved, are stored in `settings_data.json`. These are currently the only two files that reside in the `/config` directory.

*Layouts* serve as the "master template" for all pages in your theme, and as such they contain all the HTML common to every page (for example, the `<head>` section). Most themes only require the single default layout, which is called `theme.liquid`, but you can create as many base layouts as you like. If you're working with a store on Shopify Plus (Shopify's enterprise offering), you'll also have access to `checkout.liquid`, which defines the layout of the store's checkout pages.

*Locales* are JSON-formatted translation files for all the different locales (locations) your theme may support—`en.default.json`, `es.json`, etc. You're not required to provide translations for multiple languages with your theme, but it's a good idea to make sure your theme supports future internationalization. All themes being submitted for sale on the Shopify Theme Store must fully support internationalization.

*Sections* and *snippets* are similar, in that they both contain small pieces of HTML and Liquid code that can be included from other templates. Their goal is to allow you to break your theme code into smaller, logical components, making maintenance and re-use much easier. Where they differ is that sections (the newer of the two) allow you to define component-level theme settings, stylesheets, and JavaScript.

While both sections and snippets can be used "statically" by including them directly from within a theme's template files, sections have the additional ability to be dynamically included and configured on a store's home page by a merchant. We'll see detailed examples of both `sections` and `snippets` later as we walk through the details of building a theme.

*Templates* contain the HTML structure for the different types of pages in your theme— for example, `product.liquid` is used for your product pages, while `index.liquid` is used for your home page and `article.liquid` is used for blog articles. These individual page templates are rendered within the "content" section of your theme's layout file (usually `theme.liquid`).

You can create variations of each template type—e.g., `article.photo.liquid` for photo-based posts and `article.video.liquid` for video-based posts. Note that this is the only one of the top-level directories to contain a subdirectory, `/customers`, which contains several templates that are required if a store has customer login accounts enabled.

# Liquid, Shopify's Templating Language

Looking at this theme structure, you've probably noticed that lots of the files end with a .liquid extension.

Liquid is an open-source template markup language created by Shopify. Because of its nature (simple, secure, and stateless), it's a good fit for supporting dynamic content, logic, and inclusion within theme templates without sacrificing security or performance.

Like most HTML template languages that you might be familiar with (such as PHP or Ruby's ERB), we use Liquid by inserting special tags into regular HTML markup. Whereas PHP and ERB use tags that look like <?php ... ?> and <%= ... %> respectively, Liquid uses tags that look like {% ... %} (control tags) and {{ ... }} (output tags).

The Liquid code to render a list of the products inside a product collection might look like Listing 1-1.

***Listing 1-1.*** Example of Liquid Code Rendering a List of Products in a Collection

```
{% if collection.products.size > 0 %}
  <ul>
    {% for product in collection.products %}
      <li><a href="{{ product.url }}">{{ product.title | upcase }}</a></li>
    {% endfor %}
  </ul>
{% else %}
  <p>No products in collection!</p>
{% endif %}
```

We can see from this example that Liquid gives us the ability to:

- Write conditional statements like {% if ... endif %};

- Iterate over lists with {% for ... endfor %};

- Output content with {{ ... }};

- Apply filters to output like | upcase;

- Access variable objects that Shopify provides to templates like collection

Shopify's Liquid reference at `https://help.shopify.com/themes/liquid` provides a comprehensive introduction to all the tags, filters, and syntax of Liquid, but if you're like me, you'll probably find that the best way to get comfortable with Liquid is simply to dive in! Browsing through the Liquid files that come with your default theme should give you a pretty solid understanding of how things are put together. There's no need to try to have all the syntax memorized before you start—you'll quickly pick it up once you dive in.

Liquid is an open-source templating language, and it's used in many more places than just on Shopify. However, it's important to note that Shopify's implementation of Liquid contains a few Shopify-specific filters, tags, and variable objects that aren't supported by the "standard" Liquid library, so if you're wondering why a particular Liquid example is or isn't working in your Shopify theme, it's prudent to check that what you're attempting is actually possible on the platform. A handy resource for this is Shopify's Liquid Cheat Sheet at `https://www.shopify.com/partners/shopify-cheat-sheet`. It's a handy single-page reference for all the supported logic, objects, tags, and filters in Shopify themes. You may notice both in this book and in other examples across the web that Liquid control tags can be written like this: `{% ... %}` or like this: `{%- ... -%}` (with a minus symbol next to the percentage sign). Similarly, output tags can be written like this: `{{ ... }}` or like this: `{{- ... -}}`.

In terms of logic, these forms are the same. The difference between the two is how they affect any whitespace on either side of the Liquid tags. It used to be quite common for Shopify themes with lots of control flow logic and iteration to end up with large amounts of whitespace output to the browser, so the "percent-minus" form of the Liquid tags was introduced. Using this form will result in the Liquid processor stripping all whitespace from the left and right side of the Liquid tag in the resulting HTML.

My default position is to now always use the "percent-minus" format by default, unless that will interfere with how I want the output to appear. You can use whichever form you want, but just remember that outside of whitespace, the forms are logically equivalent and interchangeable while reading through example code.

## Assets

Aside from the Liquid files and the JSON configuration files (which are covered in more detail in Chapter 8), the other type of files we'll find in our theme are *asset files*.

Assets consist of images, stylesheets, JavaScript, and other resources that our theme needs to load in the browser. How we use these assets in our themes will become clearer as we walk through some examples, but there are a couple of things to note at this stage:

- All files in the `assets` directory are automatically made available and hosted via Shopify's CDN (`cdn.shopify.com`). This means they are heavily cached to improve the speed of delivery to end customers, but it also means that they won't be loaded from the same domain as our storefront (leading to the enforcement of cross-origin browser restrictions).

- To refer to an asset from within your Liquid templates, Shopify makes two filters available: `asset_url` and `asset_img_url`. Both take the name of an asset and return the URL to that asset on the CDN, with the latter allowing for some additional parameters to do things like resize or crop image assets.

- Shopify natively supports Sass precompilation for stylesheets, so you can add a `styles.scss` file directly to your `assets` directory and Shopify will compile it to CSS and make it available to your theme. (For example, you could include it in the `<head>` section of your `theme.liquid` with the Liquid `{{ 'styles.scss.css' | asset_url | stylesheet_tag }}`.)

- Shopify also supports text-based assets like JavaScript, stylesheets, or SVG images having a `.liquid` extension, which it will compile before uploading to the CDN. This means you can use Liquid control flow logic and theme settings to introduce a level of dynamic logic into your asset files. You'll see some practical examples of that in the chapters to come, especially in Chapter 8.

# Working with Shopify Themes

While Shopify themes introduce a few new concepts, they don't stray too far from the concepts of "standard" web development. At the end of the day, we're using marked-up templates, blended with a little Liquid, to generate HTML that gets pushed to the user's browser and loads in assets like images, stylesheets, and scripts. This makes Shopify theme development quite accessible to newer developers and allows you to get up and running quickly.

There are a couple of "gotchas" that can arise when coming to Shopify development for the first time though, so I thought I'd share them here.

- Shopify will aggressively cache the HTML output of your Liquid templates, meaning you can't rely on time-sensitive logic from within your Liquid templates (e.g., looking at the current time to determine whether to show or hide a product). For anything time-sensitive like this, I recommend using JavaScript.

- While Shopify supports the compilation of Sass files into CSS stylesheets, for security reasons it doesn't support the @import syntax, meaning all of your styles need to be written in the one file. The version of Sass used by Shopify is also a little older, so some newer Sass features aren't supported. For these reasons, I generally avoid using Shopify's Sass functionality and use a more advanced development workflow (discussed in the next chapter) to precompile my assets. For further detail on Shopify, Sass, and theme development, refer to Tiffany Tse's excellent three-part series *A Beginner's Guide to Sass with Shopify*.[1]

- As a Shopify theme developer, you need to be aware that it won't always be only your code running on a merchant's store. In additional to some lightweight scripts added by Shopify for admin and tracking, any Shopify apps added by a merchant may manipulate your theme's template or asset files, load additional scripts and stylesheets, or dynamically adjust your markup. While this can be frustrating, you can alleviate many issues by programming your themes defensively, making them easy to edit and maintain, and following robust development workflow practices.

## Setting Up Development Stores

To actually get started developing Shopify themes, we're going to need to create a "development store" on Shopify. This is because, unlike when we're developing with regular web sites, there's no real way to preview or test our Shopify themes locally.

---

[1]https://www.shopify.com/partners/blog/a-beginners-guide-to-building-shopify-themes-with-sass-part-1-getting-started-with-sass

Development stores function the same way as regular Shopify stores (apart from not being able to accept real payments), so they're a good testing ground. You can convert development stores to fully fledged Shopify stores with the click of a button, so it's quite common to build a store for a client as a dev store before handing it off.

Being able to create development stores just requires registering as a Shopify Partner (which you can do at `https://www.shopify.com/partners`). Registration is free and only takes a couple of minutes—once you're done, you'll be taken to the Partner Dashboard (as seen in Figure 1-3), where you can view all your existing development stores or create new ones.

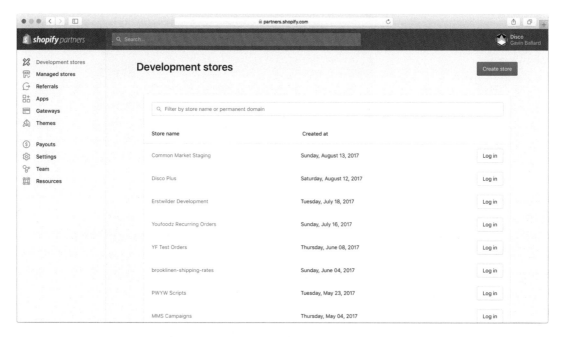

***Figure 1-3.***   *The Development Stores tab in the Partner Dashboard*

If you haven't created a development store before or poked around in the guts of a Shopify theme, this would be a great time to start! Just click Create Store from the Development Stores tab, enter some login information, and you're away.

After the store's been created, you'll be taken to the store's administration dashboard. You'll see a tab called Online Store - Themes in the left sidebar. Click it and you'll see that your store has been set up with a simple default theme named Debut.

You'll see how to sync theme files to your computer and edit them locally in Chapter 2, but for now you can get a look at how your default theme is put together by using the

Shopify Admin's built-in theme editor. You can open the editor by clicking the Actions button on the default theme, then clicking Edit HTML/CSS (See Figure 1-4).

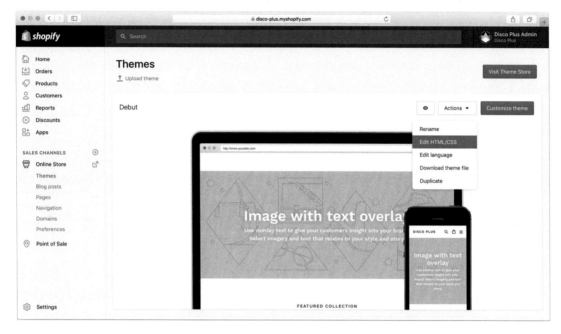

***Figure 1-4.***  *Opening the theme editor for the default Debut theme*

Spend a couple of minutes now walking through the structure of your default theme and referring to the "Anatomy of a Shopify Theme" section to make sure you're familiar with the role of each part of the theme structure. Once you've done that, you can move on to the next chapter, where you'll see how to best set yourself up for painless theme development.

# Summary

In this chapter, you've been introduced to how a Shopify theme is structured, and learned about the responsibilities of each part of that structure. You've seen that Shopify theme development shares a lot of similarities with a regular web development workflow, and this chapter highlighted the key places where they differ, including an introduction to the templating language Liquid.

Finally, you've seen how you can get started on your theme development journey by setting up a Shopify Partner account and creating a development store.

# CHAPTER 2

# Tools and Workflow

We've had an introduction to how Shopify themes are put together, and ended the last chapter looking at the contents of the default Debut theme via the Shopify Admin's online theme editor. If you were a bit of a masochist, you could do all your theme development through this editor. If you tried that, though, you'd most likely come across these difficulties:

- The online editor is nice—one of the best of its kind—but it doesn't quite compare to desktop IDEs or text editors in terms of useful development features.

- If you're familiar and productive as a web developer with a certain development environment, you lose that productivity.

- You need be online and in your browser to make any kind of change to the theme.

- Collaborating with others on the development of your theme is difficult and can easily lead to people overwriting their work.

- Your theme is stored in only one place, without any backup.

- While there is a limited form of version control (you're able to revert individual files to previous versions), there's nothing that compares to "serious" version control systems like Git or Mercurial.

- You need edit files "as is," meaning you can't easily use techniques like concatenating assets together or minifying them for production use.

This chapter looks at how to address each of these limitations by setting up a local development environment that synchronizes your code changes to Shopify. It also looks at how to use a popular revision control system (Git) to properly version and manage changes to a theme, and finally looks at advanced build tools (Shopify's Slate and others)

© Gavin Ballard 2017
G. Ballard, *The Definitive Guide to Shopify Themes*, DOI 10.1007/978-1-4842-2641-4_2

that allow us to utilize more advanced web development techniques when dealing with themes.

You don't *need* to implement these practices before starting work on a theme, but it's good to get into some of these habits sooner rather than later—I can guarantee it'll make your Shopify development experience much smoother. I do recommend that before moving on to Chapter 4, where you'll start developing your own example theme, you at least familiarize yourself with the process of editing theme files locally and having the changes automatically pushed to a Shopify store.

# Moving to Local Development

The first improvement we're going to make to our development workflow is to move where we edit our theme files from the online editor to a local machine. Getting a copy of our current theme's files is straightforward. From the Themes section of your store's admin, use the Actions dropdown and select Download theme file (see Figure 2-1).

***Figure 2-1.*** *Downloading the current theme as a .zip file*

Shopify will e-mail you a download link, which you can fetch, unzip, and move to a working directory, as in Listing 2-1.

***Listing 2-1.*** Unzipping a Downloaded Theme File and Viewing Its Contents from the Command Line

```
$ unzip ~/Downloads/example-theme.zip -d /projects/example-theme
$ cd /projects/example-theme
$ ls
assets          config          layout          locales
sections        snippets        templates
```

Now that we have a copy of the theme files locally, we're able to use a text editor or IDE of choice to develop the theme. There's no one "best" choice for an editor or toolset; really, it's up to you and what you're familiar or comfortable with. If you're stuck for ideas, popular editors include Vim, Sublime Text, and Atom.

---

**Tip** If your editor of choice supports plugins or syntax extensions, make sure you check to see if one for the Liquid templating language is available, as it will make working with Shopify theme files a much more pleasant experience. If you can't find anything to support Liquid specifically, you can try finding an extension that supports Twig (an alternate templating language with syntax very similar to Liquid) and associating `.liquid` files with it in your editor.

---

## Synchronizing Changes to Shopify

Being able to make changes in our own editor is nice and solves the first few issues identified at the start of the chapter. However, now we have another problem: how do we push any changes we make on our local files back to our Shopify store?

We could copy and paste the contents of your changed files from our local environment to the online web editor, but that hardly seems like an improvement. We could also zip up the theme directory and upload the `.zip` file through the Shopify admin, but that would be a pain if we needed to do it every time we made a change.

## Introducing Theme Kit

The solution to this problem is Theme Kit (`https://github.com/Shopify/themekit`), a small command-line utility built and maintained by Shopify. Because it's built as a simple, single cross-platform binary, developers can use it regardless of the platform they're working on. (Theme Kit was built as a replacement for the previous solution, the `shopify_theme` gem. It performed a similar function but required users to have a working copy of Ruby operating on their local machines.)

I'll leave the download and setup instructions for different platforms to Theme Kit's thorough documentation (found at `https://shopify.github.io/themekit`), but once it's set up, it will let you download and upload theme files from the command line, as seen in Listing 2-2. Even better, you can use it to watch a theme directory and automatically upload changed files as they are saved, as seen in Listing 2-3.

***Listing 2-2.*** Command-Line Example Showing Theme Kit Configuration and Download/Upload Flow

```
$ cd /projects
$ mkdir /projects/example-theme
$ cd ./example-theme
$ theme configure --store example.myshopify.com --password
905bbb49ee10d0eb9c7b380183b2bc43 --themeid 74729482
$ theme download layout/theme.liquid
[development]: 1 / 1 [================] 100 %
(... edit layout/theme.liquid ...)
$ theme upload layout/theme.liquid
[development]: 1 / 1 [================] 100 %
```

***Listing 2-3.*** Command-Line Example Showing Theme Kit Watching a Theme Directory for Changes and Uploading Them to Shopify Automatically

```
$ cd /projects/example-theme
$ theme watch
[development] Watching for changes on host example.myshopify.com
[development] Received Update event of layout/theme.liquid
[development] Successfully performed Update operation for file layout/
theme.liquid to example.myshopify.com
```

## Using Theme Kit

With Theme Kit set up and watching our files for changes, we can use the local text editor or IDE to manage and edit the theme files, then switch over to the browser and refresh to see the changes. It's not the most ideal workflow for web development (and can seem a bit clunky when compared with some modern web development workflows that allow automated and instant "hot reloading" of code in the browser), but it has a short enough feedback cycle to be practical for day-to-day development.

A couple of things to note about Theme Kit:

- It stores all configuration details (store URL, API credentials, etc.) in a file called config.yml. This file allows for the definition of different "environments" (e.g., development, staging, and production) to aid the process of updating multiple themes from a single theme directory.

- Using Theme Kit, we can skip the .zip file download step to get started working on an existing theme, just by running the theme configuration step and running theme download without any arguments from the command line.

- You're able to work on and preview themes that aren't currently published on a Shopify store (a recommended practice for sites actively being used by customers). You can do this by finding the ID of the unpublished theme in the Shopify Admin (Theme Kit's documentation has instructions on how to do this), setting it in config.yml, and running theme open to preview the theme in your default browser.

# Putting Your Theme Under Version Control

If you're not doing it already, the biggest takeaway from this lesson should be this: use a version control system (such as Git or Mercurial) when developing your themes. If you're not familiar with VCSes, the Git book provides a great overview at https://git-scm.com/book/en/v2/Getting-Started-About-Version-Control.

In the context of Shopify themes, version control:

- Stops you from making mistakes in your theme's codebase that can't be recovered from

- Makes it easier for teams to work on a theme together

- Keeps track of the work that's been done on your theme (and who's done it)

- Lets you experiment with new features on "feature" or "topic" branches, which can be tested without affecting your production code

- Provides a means to simplify the deployment of your themes in conjunction with a deployment tool (you'll see how this works in Chapter 11)

After you start using revision control for a little while, you'll also notice that the way you start thinking about your development process changes. You'll find yourself thinking about changes to your theme's codebase in terms of small, atomic chunks that are easily comprehensible to yourself, your teammates, and future developers. You can also take advantage of the wide range of tools and services in the version control ecosystem, such as GitHub, GitLab, or Bitbucket for code hosting, or tools like GitX for code review (see Figure 2-2).

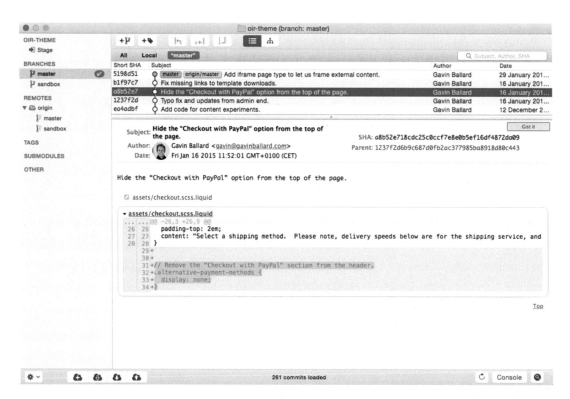

***Figure 2-2.***  *GitX, a visual Git diff tool, gives an overview of the theme's history and changes*

# A Git Workflow for Shopify Themes

Git is pretty much the de facto version control system these days (and it's the only one I'm familiar with, having managed to force unhappy memories of RCS and Subversion out of my head). If you're a Mercurial fan, I apologize but the following examples are going to be pretty Git-centric.

Assuming we have Git installed, Listing 2-4 shows how we would start putting our example theme under revision control.

*Listing 2-4.* Initializing a Git Repository in a Shopify Theme Directory

```
$ cd /projects/example-theme
$ git init .
Initialized empty Git repository in /projects/example- theme/.git/
$ echo "config.yml" > .gitignore
$ git add .
$ git commit -m "Initial commit."
```

Note that before we initialize the repository, we have to add `config.yml` to Git's ignore list. This is because Theme Kit uses this file to store sensitive API credentials, which we definitely don't want checked in to revision control. From there, you can edit the theme files locally while running the theme gem to automatically upload the changes to the store, and then once we're done, commit the changes to Git.

If you're in a situation where you're not sure if your local working directory matches what's on your Shopify store, you can run a `theme download` to fetch all of the remote files and use `git diff` to see the differences.

This actually occurs quite often for me when I'm working with clients that like to be able to make small changes (often minor copy or style tweaks) to their themes themselves through the web editor. Doing a `theme download` and committing any of their changes can avoid overwriting their work if you end up touching the same file. (If this is happening often, it's probably a good sign that the changes the client is making should be moved into a theme setting or language file, which is covered in Chapter 8.)

---

**Tip**   When you run `theme download`, sometimes you might notice some "orphan files" being pulled down from your Shopify theme—files that used to be in your repository and were renamed or deleted, but still got uploaded to the version of the theme on the Shopify servers. A nice one-line command to clean those files from the server (after you've run `theme download`) is `git clean -n | sed 's/Would remove //' | xargs theme remove`. This uses `git clean` to get a list of files that aren't in version control and passes them on to the `theme remove` command to clean them up from the server. This command won't remove the files locally, so you don't need to worry about accidentally losing work.

---

# Theme Feature Branches with Git

When using Git for development, it's quite common to want to work on a *feature branch* in order to develop a new feature without impacting the master or live codebase. With a bit of tinkering, we can do this with Shopify themes as well. Assuming that:

1.  You have a main theme currently installed and published on your Shopify store (the "master" theme).

2.  You have a local copy of that theme that's been put into version control (the "master" branch).

3.  You're synchronizing your changes to the master theme using Theme Kit and have configured Theme Kit's `config.yml` with the ID of the "master" theme.

You can create a feature branch to work on by first making sure that any `theme watch` process in Theme Kit is stopped, and then, in your browser:

1.  Open the Themes section in the store admin.

2.  Open the Actions dropdown on the "master" theme and select Duplicate

3.  Wait for the theme to duplicate, then get the ID of the newly created theme by clicking the Customize Theme button and looking at the URL.

Then, on the command line, switch to a new git branch and swap over the theme ID, as shown in Listing 2-5.

***Listing 2-5.*** Swapping to a Git Feature Branch from the Command Line

```
$ cd /project/example-theme
$ git checkout -b new-feature
Switched to a new branch 'new-feature'
$ sed -i '' 's/[master theme ID]/[new theme ID]/g' config.yml
$ theme watch
[development] Watching for changes on host example.myshopify.com
```

You've now created a completely separate preview theme on your Shopify store that will be synchronized to and from the local new-feature branch. Make some changes, wait for them to be uploaded automatically, and run `theme open`. You'll be taken to a preview of your "new-feature" theme (you'll see a notice to this effect at the bottom of your browser, as in Figure 2-3), but visitors coming to the regular site will still be looking at the "master" theme.

***Figure 2-3.*** *This overlay appears at the bottom of the browser when we're viewing a page not visible to public visitors*

If you're wondering what that `sed` command in the console was all about, it's simply updating the `config.yml` file to point to the new copy of the theme on your store instead of the master. You could do the same thing by simply opening `config.yml` in a text editor and changing the line containing `theme_id` manually.

As you can see, this process is a little tricky, and it can get even trickier when you're trying to switch back and forth between branches, as you'll often want to do. The process for switching back to working on the master branch from the feature branch would now be something like:

1. Ensure all changes we want to keep on our feature branch are committed or stashed.

2. Ensure any `theme watch` process is stopped.

3. Run `git checkout master`.

4. Edit the `theme_id` in `config.yml` file to point to the "master" theme again.

5. Run `theme watch`.

Once you've gotten used to this process, you can execute branch switches quite easily. You can also merge in changes to your master branch while `theme watch` is running and have your merged files update directly to the main Shopify store theme (watch out for merge conflicts, though!).

This workflow suits you for now, and it can handle everything we'll be throwing at it as we build the example theme in the following chapters. In Chapter 11, you'll start looking at some alternative deployment strategies for themes and learn how you can automate the rollout of theme changes to themes currently in production.

# Slate and Theme Build Tools

Up to this point, we've had a 1:1 correlation between the theme files we're editing while building our theme and the final format used by Shopify. This is great while getting started—it helps us fully understand how Shopify themes are put together and lets us start working with themes very quickly. But if you're coming from a web development background outside of Shopify, you'll understand that modern web sites rarely have this 1:1 mapping between source files and deliverables in production.

As with any other web site, Shopify themes can benefit greatly from transforming source files in different ways before delivering them to the end user. Two such transformations are *concatenation* and *optimization*.

*Concatenation* takes many separate files and bundles them together as a single asset to be sent to the browser. This allows us to logically separate and maintain files while writing our theme, but send only a single file to the browser. *Optimization* takes a source file (it could be JavaScript, CSS, Liquid, or an image) and performs some processing on it, usually to reduce the overall number of bytes to be delivered to the browser.

You'll be looking at the specifics of these processes and their advantages in a lot more detail when you get to Chapter 10 (performance), but for current purposes, the focus is on one thing: given that we want to perform these transformations on our source files, how can we slot that into our existing development workflow?

# Grunt and Gulp: Automated Task Runners

Until recently, the best choice for anyone wanting to slot preprocessing tasks like concatenation or optimization into their theme workflow was to use a *task runner,* the most common ones being **Grunt** (`http://gruntjs.com`) and **Gulp** (`http://gulpjs.com`).

These tools may be familiar to web developers working on other platforms, but if you haven't seen or used them before, the goal of both is to provide a way to define a list of automated tasks to perform in certain situations. In the context of Shopify themes, some examples of these tasks could be:

- Optimizing image assets

- Preprocessing and compiling SASS or LESS source files into a final CSS stylesheet

- Concatenating and minifying JavaScript

- Packaging up the theme as a `.zip` file for distribution

Both Grunt and Gulp allow you to define the events that trigger these automated tasks, so you can configure them to watch your theme's sources files and automatically perform processing steps when changes are saved. In the standard setup I've used for my themes in the past, the local directory where I'm working on a Shopify theme looks something like Listing 2-6.

***Listing 2-6.*** The Top-Level Directory Structure of a Theme Using Grunt for a Preprocessing Workflow

```
/.build
/theme
/Gruntfile.coffee
```

In this configuration, the top-level `/theme` directory contains the source files for my theme, arranged in a structure that makes it easy to maintain. For example, instead of being constrained to a flat directory structure with all script and stylesheet assets in the one `/assets` directory, I'll separate things out into `/assets/js/vendor`, `/assets/js/product`, `/assets/js/common`, etc. `Gruntfile.coffee` defines all the tasks to be run and rules on when to trigger them, and `/.build` contains the final "built" theme, organized in the standard directory structure expected by Shopify.

When actively developing a theme, I will run Theme Kit's `theme configure` and `theme watch` commands from within the `/.build` directory, and then the `grunt watch` command from the top-level directory. As I make changes to the template and assets contained in `/theme`, Grunt's watching task detects the changes, triggers the appropriate processing tasks, and compiles the updates to `/.build`, from where Theme Kit automatically uploads the changed files to Shopify.

The directory layout for this workflow—including setup instructions and a standard `Gruntfile.coffee` that handles a multitude of common Shopify build tasks, such as Sass compilation, JavaScript minification, image optimization, and the production of a `.zip` file suitable for upload to Shopify—is freely available at `https://github.com/discolabs/shopify-theme-scaffold`.

## Other Workflow Automation Tools

Gulp and Grunt are reasonably "low level" tools, and they require you to spend a bit of time writing configuration files and setting them up to work with Shopify. There are a couple of additional workflow automation tools that I thought I should mention here that are either are a little more "user-friendly" or are built with Shopify specifically in mind:

- *Prepos* (`https://prepros.io/`) is a cross-platform GUI tool for configuring and performing common preprocessing tasks with support for live browser reloading.

- *CodeKit* (`https://codekitapp.com/`) is similar to Prepos but Mac-only (although the developer seems to have a better sense of humor).

- *Quickshot* (`https://quickshot.readme.io`) is a command-line tool but one that is specifically targeted toward Shopify development. It supports precompilation, parallel uploads and downloads, and some nice additional features like being able to download/upload Shopify blog, page, and product content.

## Introducing Slate

In the previous section, I mentioned that tools like Grunt and Gulp were "until recently" the best option for adding automated tasks into your theme workflow. In 2017, Shopify release *Slate*, a new command-line tool specifically focused on aiding the development of Shopify themes (see Figure 2-4).

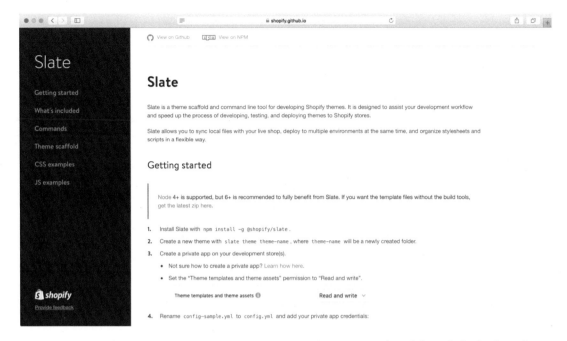

***Figure 2-4.***  *The Slate documentation page at* `https://shopify.github.io/slate`

Slate offers similar functionality to a Grunt or Gulp powered workflow: it allows you to develop Shopify themes using a flexible directory structure and slot preprocessing tasks into your development flow. It also offers some additional functionality, such as:

- Theme scaffold generation, allowing the creation of source and build directories for a new Shopify theme with a simple `slate theme new-theme` command.

- Built-in support for watching, recompiling, and uploading changes to multiple Shopify environments, meaning you only need to run a single `watch` process instead of two, as in the Grunt/Gulp and Theme Kit examples (Slate uses Theme Kit under the hood for this functionality).

- Support for live reloading of your theme in the browser, to shorten the cycle between making changes to code and seeing the results.

- Adding automated testing and style checks to your workflow.

- Providing reusable frontend components that are common to most Shopify themes.

23

Because Slate is designed specifically for Shopify theme development, it offers a smoother experience than Grunt, Gulp, or other tools. While it's still a very new addition to the Shopify ecosystem and there are some rough edges to iron out, I expect Shopify theme developers to standardize around Slate in a way we haven't seen with less standard Grunt and Gulp workflows, making it easier to share reusable theme snippets and design patterns between projects and each other.

For most of the example development in this book, we won't be using Slate or any other build tool. The reason for this is that it adds an extra layer of indirection between the code we're writing and the code running on Shopify. However, in the final chapter of the book, you will see how to move your example theme into a Slate-driven workflow, and how that plugs into a more advanced deployment process. Through the example GitHub repository, you'll see the exact code changes you make and the commands needed to use Slate with your own themes.

# Summary

This chapter covered some of the key tools you can use to develop Shopify themes and explained how they can help you build stores more efficiently. It covered local development, revision control, and workflow automation, and introduced Slate, a Shopify-developed tool that provides lots of functionality out of the box.

# CHAPTER 3

# Principles and Process

Now that we have a solid understanding of the building blocks of a Shopify theme (Chapter 1) and an understanding of how to put one together (Chapter 2), it's time to dive in and start coding, right? Almost!

The final step before we get into some practical exercises is to take a step back and think about the theme development process from a high level. What are your goals, and how can you maximize the chances of delivering a theme that successfully reaches them? What can you do to ensure your deliverables are easy to maintain, now and in six months' time?

In this chapter, I'll be discussing a few principles I like to keep in mind while working on Shopify themes, as well as looking at the sorts of processes that theme developers use to help deliver successful projects. To avoid too much fortune-cookie wisdom, I'll ground my advice in some real-world examples.

Along the way, you may feel that this chapter speaks only to freelancers and agencies building bespoke themes for clients. Don't be put off if you feel that doesn't apply to you—I believe the advice provided is equally applicable if you're building a store on your own behalf, as part of an in-house team, or with plans to make a theme available for sale in the Shopify Theme Store. In these situations, just consider yourself, your company, or Shopify merchants at large to be "the client."

## Principles of Design

The hallmark of good design is that it solves problems.

Because Shopify is an online Ecommerce platform, the problems we're tackling as theme designers most often revolve around the customer. How do we convey the "feel" of a brand in the first second of a visit? How can we make certain products more discoverable? What can we do to smooth a customer's journey through the checkout? What can we do to upsell customers and increase the average value of their cart?

© Gavin Ballard 2017
G. Ballard, *The Definitive Guide to Shopify Themes*, DOI 10.1007/978-1-4842-2641-4_3

# Understanding Design Goals

In a sense, the overarching design goal is to help maximize the revenue a store generates. (If you feel this is a little too bluntly capitalist, consider that this overall goal does encompass things like brand design, creating unique and lovable web sites, and delivering fantastic customer experiences.)

Keeping this in mind can be useful when engaging in discussions with a client (or yourself) about the goal of a feature or change. If the brief is "add a carousel to the home page" or "what if we change the color of this button," bringing the conversation back to the potential impact on the bottom line can help prioritize meaningful work and discover simpler solutions to underlying problems.

Designers in the audience will recognize the "five whys" technique in action here: given any proposed feature or change, asking "why?" five times helps uncover the root problem and relate it back to the primary goal.

Asking "why" in this manner can also uncover broader underlying goals that even clients themselves aren't consciously aware of, or at least haven't explicitly stated. This happened recently during the discovery phase for a recent client of ours. A skin care company, they were planning on launching several new brands in the Australian and New Zealand markets, with a bespoke Shopify theme being designed for each brand.

During our initial conversations and while reading through the background material, we noticed that much more emphasis was being placed on "product showcase" functionality (carousels, hero images, and long-form product detail pages) than what we would consider "traditional" Ecommerce features like product forms and checkout flows. Digging in to this, we discovered the client's expectation that a large portion of their sales would be driven by offline arrangements with retailers.

This helped us understand that one of the most important goals of the Shopify site wasn't traditional Ecommerce at all, but for it to be able to function as a marketing vehicle for sales representatives pitching potential retail partners in the field. Knowing this, we could adjust our proposal to place more emphasis on this use case and align our solution to meet the client's actual goals.

# Design for Humans

Once we've established what the design goals of a Shopify site should be, our efforts turn to building a theme to reach them. Usually, this means that your theme should be designed to help human beings (customers) achieve their goal (find something they want on the site and buy it).

Style and ornamentation should take a back seat to usability and accessibility. Adding a full-page parallax sliding carousel might look great in mockups, but its value should be balanced against increases in page load time, added navigation complexity for users, and a potential decrease in accessibility.

User interfaces and messaging should strive for clarity and helpfulness, rather than being thrown in as an afterthought. If a product can't be added to the cart because it's out of stock, return a detailed message to that effect instead of a bland alert saying "error" or "no stock". Think about ways to give users an actionable next step ("We have the blue variant in stock, would you like to purchase that instead?") instead of leaving them frustrated in a dead end.

The needs of the user (clear navigation and page structure and fast page loads and response times) should be prioritized over the wants of the merchant (on-page advertising, reams of third-party tracking codes, and intrusive upsells).

Try to avoid excluding users - make your themes accessible and in compliance with standards like WAI-ARIA (`https://www.w3.org/TR/wai-aria`). Not only is this considerate and maximizes the number of people able to buy things from your store, but a failure to do so can in some cases have legal ramifications.[1]

There are a couple of nice things about championing the experience of the user like this when putting together a theme. First, it can help you focus your use cases and discussions around real people instead of platonic ideals. Second, caring deeply about your customers' experiences pays dividends in other areas: fast, painless purchases encourage repeat business, motivate word-of-mouth referrals, and (as you'll see in Chapter 9) have a positive impact on search engine rankings.

---

[1]The leading cited example of this is that of Target, who settled a USD $6 million lawsuit brought against them to failing to make their online store accessible to blind customers. See `https://www.w3.org/WAI/bcase/target-case-study`.

# Design for Different Contexts

While we haven't all been uploaded to the cloud just yet, the level of Internet connectivity for the average Western consumer has certainly increased in the last few years; so too the myriad of means to connect, whether at home on a traditional desktop/laptop, on the move from one of a bewildering array of mobile devices, or via emerging platforms like integrated messaging apps or Internet-enabled fridges.

Any of these could be relevant to an Ecommerce store, depending on the merchant and its typical customers. As a Shopify theme designer, you need to start considering the wide variety of use cases customers might have when accessing a store and the situations in which they are doing so.

Note that I'm stressing design for different *contexts*, not just different devices. This is because it's important to not only think about *which* devices your customers might be using, but *when* they're doing it and *what* they want to achieve.

Take a visitor landing on an apparel boutique's home page as an example.

- Are they on their desktop at work during their lunch break, browsing collections for fashion inspiration?

- Are they sitting on the couch with a glass of wine and their mobile that evening, making an impulse buy of the shirt they saw earlier that day?

- Are they using the same mobile, but in the middle of rush hour trying to find the store's nearest physical location before closing time?

It's usually impossible to spend the time and effort required to build a site that optimizes for all scenarios simultaneously, but a good designer will take the time to identify these different potential use cases and work with the client to prioritize them.

# Principles of Development

Once you move out of the design phase and start the development of your theme, there are a couple of things you can bear in mind to make the deliverables you produce robust and maintainable.

It's not always easy to prioritize these things, especially when we're up against a deadline or trying to justify some extra hours to a client. They do tend to take a little extra time upfront, but in my experience, they more than pay for themselves in the long run.

# Keep It Simple

The simpler the concepts and code in your theme are, the easier it is to write and maintain them. For your code, this can mean:

- Keeping the number of included Liquid snippets to a minimum to simplify your code's mental model

- Breaking clever Liquid one-liners down into smaller, easier-to-understand steps

- Preferring HTML and Liquid over JavaScript to drive dynamic logic

- Identifying pages or components that are defined in different places but serve the same purpose and considering combining them into one

---

**Note**   Development practices that allow breaking your source code down into small, logical components can be a huge help here. You saw some examples of this in Chapter 2 ("Tools and Workflow") and will encounter more in Chapter 11 ("Collaborative Theme Development").

---

It can also help to focus on leveraging Shopify's built-in features and concepts like collections, products, linked lists, and tags, rather than trying to develop your own. Understanding the limitations of Liquid and Shopify and working within those boundaries reduces headaches versus clever hacks to work around them.

On a related note, I try to avoid relying on Shopify apps for common Ecommerce functionality whenever I can. Not only is there an ongoing financial cost for the use of apps, many of them demand complex Liquid code changes and extra JavaScript, adding mental and performance overhead as well. Many Shopify apps are well-written, robust pieces of software that won't interfere with a store's theme or other apps—but many aren't, and that can lead to all sorts of issues down the track.

To give an example, I'll commonly see merchants and developers relying on an app for simple Upsell functionality, such as "if a customer has product A in their cart, suggest they add product B". While several apps can handle this and more complex scenarios, most rely on JavaScript to examine and adjust the cart (meaning an extra script file to load and a delay for the user) and in some situations, force a full-page refresh on the user. Compare that to the simplicity of the Liquid snippet in Listing 3-1, which displays a configurable upsell message based on the current contents of a customer's cart.

***Listing 3-1.*** A Simple Liquid Implementation of a Configurable Upsell Message on the Cart Page

```liquid
<!-- templates/cart.liquid -->
{%- unless settings.upsell_trigger_product == blank or settings.upsell_
target_product == blank -%}
{%- assign has_trigger_product = false -%}
  {%- assign has_target_product = false -%}

  {%- comment -%}
    Iterate over items currently in the cart to see if we have our trigger
    product but not the target product.
  {%- endcomment -%}
  {%- for item in cart.items -%}
    {%- if item.product == settings.upsell_trigger_product -%}
      {%- assign has_trigger_product = true -%}
    {%- endif -%}
    {%- if item.product == settings.upsell_target_product -%}
      {%- assign has_target_product = true -%}
    {%- endif -%}
  {%- endfor -%}

  {%- if has_trigger_product and !has_target_product -%}
  <p>
    Why not <a href="{{ settings.upsell_target_product.url }}">
      add a {{ settings.upsell_target_product.title }}?
    </a>
  </p>
  {%- endif -%}
{%- endunless -%}
```

# Utilize Progressive Enhancement

As web designers, we often want to make use of the latest and greatest features browsers have to offer. However, it's important to make sure that we don't leave segments of visitors behind—especially in the context of Shopify themes, where that exclusion translates directly to lost dollars.

*Progressive enhancement* is the practice of designing web sites with a "bottom-up" approach—starting with something that works for devices with the most basic capabilities (say, a monochrome Kindle browser with no JavaScript and limited graphics support), then "progressively" leveraging more advanced features (JavaScript! CSS3! Push notifications! Color!) when available.

Using this approach doesn't necessarily take more effort during the development phase, and it can help us avoid situations where entire groups of potential customers are denied the opportunity to buy something. (The list of high-profile failures in this regard is sobering—examples include visitors to Nike.com being presented with a black screen unless their browser supported a specific CSS feature; and perhaps more egregiously, for a long time, Walmart's Add to Cart button didn't even display for users without JavaScript!).[2]

---

**Note**   We'll be using a progressive enhancement approach to all the code we develop as part of the practical part of this book, with a focus on accessibility support and ensuring your themes provide a solid fallback experience for users without JavaScript—two of the most important concerns for Ecommerce stores.

---

# Document Things

A big mistake beginning Shopify theme developers make (that I was guilty of myself, in spades) is focusing too much on the initial delivery of a Shopify site and not enough on everything that comes after a successful launch.

If everything goes to plan and the site using your theme sticks around, then new seasons, product lines, competitors, and industry trends will demand iteration and wholesale changes. Whether it's yourself or another developer tasked with making those

---

[2]These examples are taken from the Filament Group's book *Designing with Progressive Enhancement* by Todd Parker, Patty Toland, Scott Jehl, and Maggie Costello Wachs.

changes, properly documenting code, processes and architecture can make everyone's life that much easier.

For code, this means taking the time to cleanly structure your Liquid, JavaScript, and stylesheets and add thorough, meaningful comments to them.

Compare the Liquid snippet in Listing 3-2 with the snippet in Listing 3-3, both of which do the same thing. How much extra time and energy would you need to spend mentally untangling what the first example is doing compared with the second? How confident would you be making changes to each of them?

***Listing 3-2.*** A Difficult-to-Parse Liquid Snippet for Calculating Related Products

```
{%- assign p1s = -1 -%}{%- assign p2s = -1 -%}{%- assign p3s = -1 -%}
{%- assign p4s = -1 -%}
{%- for cp in collections.all.products -%}
{%- unless cp.id == product.id -%}
{%- assign cp_score = 0 -%}
{%- for tag in product.tags -%}{%- for rt in cp.tags -%}
{%- if tag == rt -%}
{%- assign cp_score = cp_score | plus: 1 -%}
{%- endif -%}
{%- endfor -%}{%- endfor -%}
{%- if cp_score > p1s -%}{%- assign p1s = cp_score -%}
{%- assign p1h = cp.handle -%}
{%- elsif cp_score > p2s -%}{%- assign p2s = cp_score -%}
{%- assign p2h = cp.handle -%}
{%- elsif cp_score > p3s -%}{%- assign p3s = cp_score -%}
{%- assign p3h = cp.handle -%}
{%- elsif cp_score > p4s -%}{%- assign p4s = cp_score -%}
{%- assign p4h = cp.handle -%}
{%- endif -%}
{%- endunless -%}
{%- endfor -%}
<div class="row">
{%- for rp in collections.all.products -%}{%- if rp.handle == p1h or
rp.handle == p2h or rp.handle == p3h or rp.handle == p4h -%}
```

```
<div class="col-md-4">{%- include 'product' with rp -%}</div>
{%- endif -%}{%- endfor -%}
</div>
```

***Listing 3-3.*** A Liquid Snippet Doing the Same Job as Listing 3-2, but in a Much More Maintainable Fashion

```
{%- comment -%}
  Calculated related products using similar tags as a simple scoring system.
{%- endcomment -%}

{%- assign product_1_score = -1 -%}
{%- assign product_2_score = -1 -%}
{%- assign product_3_score = -1 -%}
{%- assign product_4_score = -1 -%}

{%- for current_product in collections.all.products -%}
  {%- unless current_product.id == product.id -%}

  {%- assign current_product_score = 0 -%}

  {%- for tag in product.tags -%}
    {%- for related-tag in current_product.tags -%}
      {%- if tag == related-tag -%}
        {%- assign current_product_score = current_product_score | plus: 1 -%}
      {%- endif -%}
    {%- endfor -%}
  {%- endfor -%}

  {%- if current_product_score > product_1_score -%}
    {%- assign product_1_score = current_product_score -%}
    {%- assign product_1_handle = current_product.handle -%}
  {%- elsif current_product_score > product_2_score -%}
    {%- assign product_2_score = current_product_score -%}
    {%- assign product_2_handle = current_product.handle -%}
  {%- elsif current_product_score > product_3_score -%}
    {%- assign product_3_score = current_product_score -%}
    {%- assign product_3_handle = current_product.handle -%}
```

```
{%- elsif current_product_score > product_4_score -%}
  {%- assign product_4_score = current_product_score -%}
  {%- assign product_4_handle = current_product.handle -%}
{%- endif -%}

{%- endunless -%}
{%- endfor -%}
<div class="row">
{%- for related-product in collections.all.products -%}
  {%- if related-product.handle == product_1_handle or related-product.
  handle == product_2_handle or related-product.handle == product_3_handle
  or related-product.handle == product_4_handle -%}
    <div class="col-md-4">
      {%- include 'product' with related-product -%}
    </div>
  {%- endif -%}
{%- endfor -%}
</div>
```

Good documentation doesn't only have to be in code, either. Some other things that can help are:

- Documenting the concepts and architecture of your theme in a README file in your source code.

- Writing a "getting started" guide for others with step-by-step instructions on setting up a development environment, walking through any non-standard aspects of your theme and highlighting any "gotchas."

- Providing clients and store owners with a "content management guide," with instructions on how they can manage various aspects of their Shopify theme without relying on a developer. Following the principle of "show, don't tell," I often like to record short screencasts for this purpose.

# Use Defensive and Modular Programming

*Programming defensively* means that we try to make as few assumptions as possible in our code and handle failure gracefully. In the context of Shopify themes:

- Avoid writing code that fails if a DOM element is not present on the page or if a specific Liquid template isn't being used. Other third-party code, apps, or developers may have adjusted the theme.

- When assigning variables in your Liquid code, try to use unique variable names to avoid overriding common names that other code may rely on (e.g., use `{% assign first_related_product ... %}` instead of `{% assign product ... %}`).

- For JavaScript, don't assume the presence of jQuery or other libraries if they aren't directly under your control. Fall back to loading them yourself from within your script if you must, but avoid writing code that loads eight different versions of jQuery (yes, I've seen it happen).

- Also for JavaScript, avoid writing code that requires a specific order of execution or that needs to be executed at the top of the page. Doing this not only avoids a lot of common functional problems with your code, but will also make it much easier to build performant themes (see Chapter 10).

With *modular programming*, we try to break our theme down into small, independent components with a single logical function. This reduces the amount of knowledge we need to keep in our head at one time to a minimum, and makes changing the code easier. It also lets us re-use those components elsewhere in the theme with a minimum of fuss.

As a practical example of this, consider Figure 3-1, a product page in a Shopify theme that handles dynamic shipping destinations, currencies, and variant options.

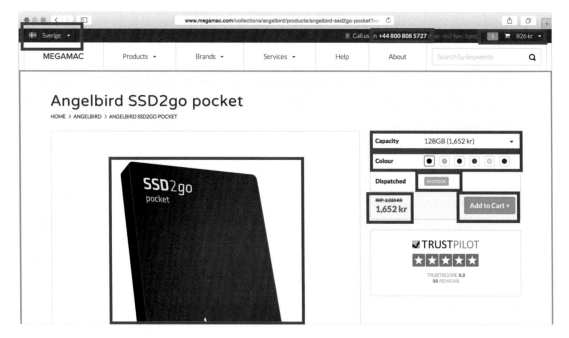

**Figure 3-1.**  *A Shopify product page with several dynamic page elements outlined*

When the destination country, customer currency, or a product option is changed by the customer, various page updates might need to be made (the feature image, the customer support number in the header, the displayed price, etc.). We could handle this with one large callback function in JavaScript that managed updating everything on the page, but a neater solution is to break down each of the boxes on the page into their own independent component that listens for relevant events and focuses only on updating itself.

This approach allows us to write small bits of code like Listing 3-4, which handles updating the displayed price element whenever the selected variant or currency changes.

**Listing 3-4.**  A Modularized JavaScript Function for the Product Page in Figure 3-1

```
$(document).on('variant.changed currency.changed', function(e, variant,
currency) {
  var formattedPrice = Currency.format(variant.price, currency);
  $('[data-variant-price]').text(formattedPrice);
});
```

If you ever want to change the way that the displayed price is rendered, you can do that in this snippet of code without worrying about affecting anything else. Likewise, if you want to change the way the `variant changed` or `currency changed` events are triggered, you can do that without having to know anything about the implementation of this price component.

# Principles of Process

No two theme building processes are going to be the same—every designer, developer, and agency is going to approach things their own way, and even within that you'll see variation depending on the client or project.

Without the possibility of a single prescriptive guideline for a winning Shopify theme development process, what I've tried to do in this section is identify four important things that I've seen successful developers commonly focus on.

## Client and Project Match

Projects where you and the client are comfortable with each other and feel like you're collaborating rather than undertaking a transaction generally see much better results. Make sure you spend some time upfront getting to know the client and what they're after before committing to a project.

Ask yourself questions like these:

- Do I feel comfortable talking to the client? Do I get on well with them?

- Am I motivated by what the client does?

- Is the project interesting on a technical level?

- Will my opinion and expertise be valued, or am I seen as "just a pair of hands"?

- Most importantly—do I feel like delivering this project will result in success for the client?

Depending on the situation, you may be in a position where you feel you should say yes despite a sense that the project isn't right for you or the client. While you need to make your own judgment calls, my experience (and the experience of many others in the industry) is that your gut instinct is often accurate and such relationships and projects falter.

# Iterative Development and Client Investment

For the clients you do end up working with, it's important to make sure that they are closely involved with the design and development of the theme along the way. Kicking off a project, disappearing for three months, and coming back with a "finished" product is a sure-fire way to deliver something the client doesn't want, need, or feel invested in.

You do need to drive and manage your development process to avoid being micromanaged by the client, but ensure that the process includes plenty of *structured* ways for your client to give feedback, discuss use cases, and test possible design options. A common technique is to plan design and development in short (one to two week) "sprints" or "cycles," with each sprint or cycle having its own specific goals and opportunities for you to present progress and receive feedback.

Planning for an iterative approach upfront also makes it easier to factor inevitable changes into your timelines and budget, and ultimately makes it more likely that you can deliver something that meets the client's needs. Having the clients regularly involved in the feedback and iteration process also gives them a greater sense of ownership in the final product.

# Expectation Setting

The culprit for many projects and client relationships gone bad is poor expectation setting. This is sometimes due to poor communication from the client, but most of the time it's freelancers or agencies that haven't been clear about the nature of deliverables, what the timeline for them is, where the scope and boundaries of a project are, and what the breakdown of responsibilities are.

A good development process should present the client with such a breakdown, clearly delineating things that are in-scope (e.g., a code for a polished theme that matches the developed mockups and wireframes) and things that aren't (e.g., the data entry of 5,000 SKUs into the Shopify backend). Timelines should be set in a way that's realistic and that account for the time needed for parties to provide feedback, conduct research, and handle revisions to the original scope.

Finally, it must be noted that expectations aren't a one-way street. It's important that you make it clear to clients what your expectations are of them, whether it's providing timely feedback on your latest iteration, sending over copy and images, or payment of invoices. For each of these expectations, be clear about the consequences on timelines and deliverables of failing to meet them.

# User Testing

Regardless of store or project size, one of the most useful yet most often overlooked things to do is user testing—getting actual people to sit down and use your theme. Without any hard data to back this up, my suspicion for the reason behind this neglect is that the expected (indeed, the desired) outcome of user testing is more work—fixing user experience issues you weren't previously aware of.

The solution is simple—plan and budget for it as part of your process, making room in your timeline (and in your ego) for addressing issues brought about by your theme's assumptions around usability.

The simplest form of user testing (and really, there's no excuse for not doing this even on a shoestring budget) is the "coffee shop or office coworker" test. Find someone who's never seen your site before, sit them in front of a desktop or mobile device, and give them a task to complete like "find a sweater you like and buy it" or "find all shoes from a particular designer." Watch over their shoulder, take copious notes (record the sessions if possible) and, above all, bite your tongue and do not help them. No design survives first contact with actual users, and I can guarantee you'll be exposed to a number of usability issues you weren't previously aware of.

For larger projects, you may want to invest the time and money in professional user testing, either by engaging a company specializing in it or by using an online user testing service. Using such services can be advantageous over the less formal "over the shoulder" approach, as they help you conduct the testing at scale while also selecting a demographic that more accurately reflects your store's visitor makeup.

Finally, once you deploy your theme, you can keep an eye on the actual visitors coming to your site to identify potential usability problems. In a recent project, we made some customizations to the Shopify checkout flow, collecting some additional information from customers on the way. The changes were quite significant, both on the frontend and also in terms of the resulting data flowing through to a third-party logistics system, so we took a pretty cautious approach to deployment. The first step was to conduct thorough testing of the frontend using the "over the shoulder" approach and with a range of different browsers and devices.

We then conducted a live test of the changes for an hour and recorded the actions of every single user session going through the checkout flow with user analytics tool Hotjar (`https://www.hotjar.com`). Reverting, we could then go through every recording to see exactly how users were interacting with the new interface and where they were getting stuck or delayed.

This method picked up a couple of usability issues that were obvious once we saw them but just hadn't cropped up until contact with real customers. One of the most obvious is shown in Figure 3-2. The clickable area of a new button design was smaller than the visual area of the button, meaning a lot of users were failing to activate it properly and consequently move to the next checkout step.

**Figure 3-2.** *The clickable area (green/darker) of one of our custom checkout buttons before user testing (left) and after correction (right)*

# Summary

In this chapter, we took a step back to think holistically about Shopify design and the goals we're trying to achieve when building a theme. The chapter discussed the importance of empathizing with the user and the importance of designing for visitors in a range of contexts.

It also discussed a number of best practices to keep in mind during the development of your themes and studied some techniques to help you uncover usability issues during the testing phase.

# CHAPTER 4

# Designing Theme Foundations

Over the next four chapters, we'll be walking through the process of designing and building an example Shopify theme—page by page, feature by feature. In this chapter, we'll be looking at the options for getting started with a new theme, then design and implement the key elements common to your store's entire site—the layout and navigation.

The focus will be on the fundamentals of building a Shopify theme more than the fundamentals of web or visual design. This means you won't see too much attention paid to styling, visual tweaks, or frontend framework choices, except for when those things directly overlap with some Shopify-specific concerns.

When building an Ecommerce site, there are a wide range of design choices that can and should be made in different scenarios—what style of navigation to use, what the best layout for a product page is, etc. The "right" choice (if there is such a thing) will of course be different depending on the store and audience in question.

We can't explore every possible choice in detail within the scope of a single book, so instead when faced with these choices, I'll discuss the different possible approaches before settling on a common one for demonstration purposes.

Also, rather than try to dump all the code used to build the example theme directly in this book, I've made it available in a GitHub repository (`https://github.com/gavinballard/defguide-theme`). The commit history of this repository tracks the progress of the example theme from this chapter onward, so it's easy for you to follow along with the exact changes made at each section.

I will use code in the text when it's helpful to illustrate a point or demonstrate a technique. To keep these examples as clear and as useful as possible, I'll strip them of extraneous information (like HTML class names or accessibility attributes). You can

© Gavin Ballard 2017
G. Ballard, *The Definitive Guide to Shopify Themes*, DOI 10.1007/978-1-4842-2641-4_4

always refer to the corresponding snippets of code in the example theme repository, which contain things in full.

Ready? Let's get started!

# A Starting Point

Before we start designing and building our theme, let's establish the workflow and get into a position to begin work. I discussed a variety of tools and workflow techniques in Chapter 2, including Shopify's Slate and other build tools that assemble your themes into Shopify's expected directory structure from a different starting point.

Learning about and using these tools is important, but to begin with you're going to strike a balance between simplicity and ease-of-use. This assumes that we're working directly with the Shopify theme directory structure (so **no** build and compilation tools like Grunt or Slate), but **are** working on files locally with a text editor and using Theme Kit or the Theme gem to keep changes synced with a development store (refer back to Chapter 2 if you need a refresher on either of these tools).

# Theme Scaffolds

In your day-to-day life dealing with Shopify themes, much of your work will be done on existing Shopify source files—perhaps you'll be brought in to customize a theme purchased from the theme store or developed by someone else. For situations where you're starting on a "greenfield" project, it's helpful to have a starting point—a blank canvas to work from. There are several freely available theme scaffolds:

- *Slate*: Shopify's official theme development tool includes its own default theme setup, which will be generated when you run `slate theme new-theme-name`. It's a reasonably bare-bones setup, giving you template files and several initial styles and JavaScript helpers. Slate uses a series of build tools to "compile" your theme from a source directory.

- *Timber*: Before Slate came on the scene, this was Shopify's official theme framework, offering many styling helpers and JavaScript functionality like Ajax carts. With the introduction of Slate, Timber is no longer being maintained so it may be best to look at Timber as inspiration for how to implement particular Shopify features rather than as a starting point.

- *Shopify Theme Scaffold*: This is an unofficial project, based on the theme work we do at Disco. It includes a simple Grunt-based workflow for theme compilation. Unlike the tools, it's truly a blank canvas, as it includes empty template files and no styling or JavaScript.

Over time, you'll probably start to develop your own preferences for working with Shopify themes and start to build your own starting scaffold.

For the purposes of this book, however, we're going right back to basics. We're going to start by uploading `blank.zip` (available from the GitHub resources for this book) into the Theme Editor on our development store. As its name suggests, `blank.zip` is a completely empty theme that contains only the bare minimum required for Shopify to consider it a valid upload. You can see in Figure 4-1 that, once it's uploaded, it lives up to that name.

***Figure 4-1.*** *You can upload the blank.zip file directly into the Themes page in the Shopify admin (left). Once you've done that, previewing the theme provides an exciting view (right)*

# Sample Product Data

A common design mistake is to build around unrealistic "dummy" data (lorem ipsum, anyone?), rather than the actual content that will be used on your site in production. One habit I encourage all theme developers to foster is ensuring that clients provide them with actual product data and copy before starting out on a theme build.

This isn't always possible, but fortunately Shopify provides a series of dummy store inventories that you can import to a development store to help you work with realistic data. The dummy products contain a variety of images with different dimensions, number of variants, and descriptions of various lengths so that your theme can be properly tested across a range of content.

You can download one of the four sets of sample product data from `https://github.com/shopifypartners/shopify-product-csvs-and-images`.[1]

---

### EXERCISE: A STARTING POINT

1. Set up a Shopify Development store to start following along with the practical exercises. Refer to Chapter 1 for the steps involved.

2. Download `blank.zip` from the book's resources page and upload it to your store from the Themes page in the Shopify Admin.

3. Download one of the sets of sample product data from Shopify and import it into your store.

4. Following the steps outlined in Chapter 2 under "Moving to Local Development," download a copy of the blank theme to your local machine and use Theme Kit to ensure that any changes you make locally are synchronized to your Shopify store.

5. An optional (but highly recommended) step is to place your theme under revision control, so that you can save your progress along the way and compare it to the commit history of the example theme on GitHub. Follow the steps in Chapter 2 under "Putting Your Theme Under Revision Control" for the steps involved here.

---

[1]Instructions on importing the product data can be found at `https://www.shopify.com/partners/blog/93467590-design-your-store-faster-with-product-csvs-and-images`.

# Your Theme's Layout

Unless they specify otherwise, all of the page templates in your theme will be rendered inside the default layout, theme.liquid. The layout file that comes with the blank starting theme looks like Listing 4-1.

***Listing 4-1.*** The Contents of a default theme.liquid

```
<!DOCTYPE html>
<html>
  <head>
    {{ content_for_header }}
    {{ 'styles.css' | asset_url | stylesheet_tag }}
  </head>
  <body>
    {{ content_for_layout }}
    {{ 'theme.js' | asset_url | script_tag }}
  </body>
</html>
```

The overall structure should look familiar to anyone who's worked with HTML before. The Shopify-specific elements are:

- {{ content_for_header }}: Shopify requires placing this output tag inside your layout's <head> section. It'll use this location to add Shopify-side JavaScript, styles, and tracking code on every page rendered on your storefront.

- {{ content_for_layout }}: Shopify requires placing this output tag inside your layout's <body> section. This will be where the content for each of your individual page templates (page.liquid, article. liquid, etc.) will be rendered.

- `{{ 'styles.css' | asset_url | stylesheet_tag }}` and `{{ 'theme.js' | asset_url | script_tag }}`: These tags aren't strictly required, but I've included them in the default layout as you'll always want your site-wide stylesheet and scripts added on every page. `asset_url` and `stylesheet_tag` / `script_tag` are Liquid filters that convert the name of a particular asset (`'theme.js'`) first into a reference to that asset on Shopify's CDN, and then to a HTML tag that will load that asset, e.g., `<script src="//cdn.shopify.com/s/files/1/1744/7651/t/2/assets/theme.js?23317239576525266606" type="text/javascript"></script>`.

As time goes on, we'll be adding more and more content to `theme.liquid`. Much of this will be content or elements we want to appear on every page, while some will be loaded conditionally dependent on the current page template. To start with, we're going to look at the design considerations and implementation of the overall site layout and navigation elements—things that generally affect all pages of a site.

# Designing Layout and Navigation

Designing the layout and navigation of a Shopify site is about a lot more than just setting up a nice-looking navigation bar at the top of your site and making sure the dropdowns work. It's a matter of thinking about the users of your site, and how you can best help them find what they're looking for in the minimum number of steps.

When it comes to site layout, one of the tensions theme designers face is "convention versus creativity." Customers' expectations on how particular Ecommerce sites should look and operate have been shaped over time, meaning we tend to see a convergence in the appearance of Ecommerce sites. A look at the layout of the "prototypical Ecommerce site" in Figure 4-2 and you'd probably agree that 90% of Ecommerce sites fall into this basic structure.

***Figure 4-2.***   *The prototypical Ecommerce site layout*

I don't think this convergence is necessarily a bad thing. If our site follows a customer's expectations, they'll be able to find what they're looking for more efficiently, which is one of your jobs as a designer. We still have plenty of scope for finding a brand's "voice" within these conventions.

For this example theme, we're going to implement something very like the "prototypical" layout from Figure 4-2: a layout with a header section consisting of a logo and text links on the left, with a search bar, account information, and cart link on the right. Underneath that, we'll leave space for the individual page content before adding a footer at the bottom with links to the various parts of the site.

Because we anticipate lots of mobile visitors (more than half of all visits to Shopify sites are on mobile), we'll need to make sure that the layout works responsively and is easily usable on mobile by collapsing navigation items, creating large touch areas, and adjusting font sizes.

# The Site Header

For the example theme, we're going to add a new `header.liquid` section (see Listing 4-2) that renders the store name and iterates over the links defined in the main navigation menu (configurable from the Shopify Admin) as well as the Search, Log In/My Account, and Cart links. We'll then include it in the `theme.liquid` (see Listing 4-3) so that it appears on every page of the site.

***Listing 4-2.*** A Simple sections/header.liquid Section

```
<nav>

  <a href="/">{{ shop.name | escape }}</a>

  <ul>
    {%- for link in linklists.main-menu.links -%}
    <li>
      <a href="{{ link.url }}">{{ link.title | escape }}</a>
    </li>
    {%- endfor -%}
  </ul>

  <ul>
    <li class="nav-item">
      <a class="nav-link" href="/search">Search</a>
    </li>
    {%- if shop.customer_accounts_enabled -%}
      {%- if customer -%}
        <li>
          <a href="/account">{{ customer.first_name | escape }}</a>
        </li>
      {%- else -%}
        <li>
          <a href="/account/login">Log in</a>
        </li>
      {%- endif -%}
    {%- endif -%}
```

```
    <li>
      <a href="/cart">Cart ({{ cart.item_count }})</a>
    </li>
  </ul>

</nav>
```

***Listing 4-3.*** Include the Header Section at the Top of theme.liquid So That It Appears on Every Page

```
...
<body>
  {%- section 'header' -%}
  {{ content_for_layout }}
  ...
```

When rendered on the Shopify site, it looks something like Figure 4-3 (note that I've skipped the addition of all the styling code in this book; refer to the example theme repository for details). Note that the items in the menu bar (Shop, Best Sellers, etc.) are defined in the Online Store ➤ Navigation section of the Shopify Admin, not directly in the theme.

***Figure 4-3.*** *The example theme's header*

Simple, but effective! Some things to note:

- The implementation is consistent. We're not changing the menu items available or the layout of menu items depending on the current page. It's important to keep the navigation structure of the site consistent from one page to the next, as it reduces the amount of information a user must process when moving from one page to the other. Making large "contextual" changes to site layout or structure can be confusing for users and should be avoided.

- A cart link is included in its conventional spot (the top right of the page). Keeping this element means that no matter where they are, the customers know how to take the most important step on any Ecommerce site—move to the checkout. Note also that the number of items currently bagged is displayed to help the customers keep track of their cart state.

- The design allows for only a single level of navigation in the header. There are no dropdown menus or category filters at this stage. You'll be learning about navigation patterns in more detail shortly.

## Making the Header Configurable

One of the advantages of using a section for the header rather than a snippet is that we can define configuration settings directly in the section and have them appear in a simple interface in the Shopify Admin's theme customizer. To demonstrate, let's make a change to allow the storeowners to select which navigation menu they would like to use to render the list of links at the top of the site (it's currently fixed to main-menu, which is a default Shopify navigation menu).

We can start this by adding a {% schema %} definition at the top of sections/ header.liquid, then updating the way we fetch the navigation menu to use (see Listing 4-4). When this is done, users opening the theme customizer from the Shopify backend will be able to pick which menu to use (see Figure 4-4). Note that the link_list type refers to Navigation Menus, as titled in the Shopify Admin.

***Listing 4-4.*** *Addition of {% schema %} Markup*

```
{% schema %}
{
  "name": "Header",
  "settings": [
    {
      "id": "primary_link_list",
      "type": "link_list",
      "label": "Primary navigation menu",
      "default": "main-menu"
    }
  ]
}
```

```
{% endschema %}
<nav>
  ...

  {%- assign primary_link_list = linklists[section.settings.primary_link_
  list] -%}
  {%- unless primary_link_list == blank -%}
  <ul>
    {%- for link in primary_link_list.links -%}
    ...
```

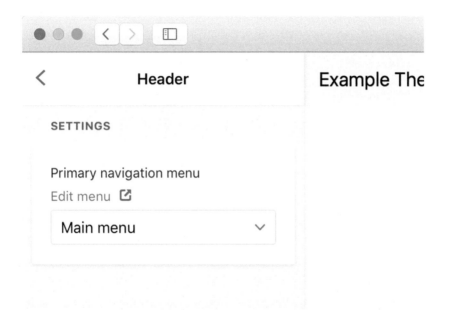

***Figure 4-4.*** *Adding the {% schema %} markup gives users a nice UI to make configuration changes inside the Shopify Admin's theme customizer*

## The Navigation Menu

The initial approach to a navigation header offers only a single level of options. For stores with a very limited number of pages or products, this simple approach may suffice. However, there are many stores where it's useful to give users more choice and a quicker way of narrowing down the product range. This is usually achieved by adding contextual menu options (e.g., dropdown menus).

# Navigation Menu Design

Picking the right menu design option for your site requires a deep understanding of the information hierarchy of the site, especially the product hierarchy. You need to consider things like the following:

- How the client/storeowner categorizes their products

- How competitors categorize the same or similar products

- How customers categorize products

- Whether the categories are "deep" (fewer top-level categories, with lots of subcategories and sub-subcategories) or "broad" (more top-level categories with fewer or no subcategories)

- The level to which categories overlap

- The facets of the products that need to be filtered or searched on

- Whether the site is "content-heavy" (e.g., contains a large number of blog posts and articles)

This list can be a bit daunting, but it's an important thing to consider when working out what sort of scale your navigation menus need. If the store only sells 2-3 products, you can skip categorization altogether; if it sells 50, you'll probably be fine with just categories; and if it sells 500+, you're going to need at least two levels of categorization.

It's important here to be aware of the (oft-lamented) limitations of the Shopify backend when it comes to categorization. Strictly speaking, we're only allowed one "real" level of categorization ("Collections" in Shopify parlance). There's no inherent notion of a subcategory. What we do get instead are a couple of different fields on products that allow us to group them: Tags, Product Types, and Product Vendors. *Tags* are most often used to approximate subcategory functionality.

My general advice in almost every area of Shopify development is to avoid being too clever and that pushing the boundaries too far leads to trouble. As a corollary to that, I don't recommend trying to implement sub-subcategories with Shopify unless you have a very clear need and a maintainable approach (perhaps with application support).

For the example store, I'm using the "Apparel" sample product data provided by Shopify. This gives us an inventory of 25 products, covering some clothing (men's and women's), bags, and some accessories. Given the spread of products and how the customers are likely to think about them, I'm going to work with four primary product categories for this store: Mens, Womens, Bags, and Accessories. As each of these categories will only have 4-5 products in them, I'm not going to subcategorize them just yet.

In addition to this product hierarchy, I'm going to work on the assumption that there are several content pages considered important by the storeowner—About, Reviews, and Press. I'd also like to provide customers a shortcut to get to the most popular products, which we could do through a link to a Best Sellers collection. Based on this information, the final example information hierarchy for the main navigation menu looks like this:

- Shop
    - Womens
    - Mens
    - Bags
    - Accessories
- Best Sellers
- About
- Reviews
- Press

Once we have a hierarchy together, we need to decide how to best implement that on the storefront. Given that Shopify doesn't natively support hierarchical navigation menus (yet—at the time of writing, this feature is in beta), the standard way to implement these is to:

1. Create a new Navigation menu in the Shopify Admin for each submenu, with a name matching its top-level name (in this example, this would mean creating a new navigation menu called Shop that contained links to the Womens, Mens, Bags, and Accessories collections).

2. While iterating through the top-level menu items, update the Liquid code to check to see if a submenu exists for the current item. If so, render that submenu by iterating over its items in turn.

You can see how I've implemented this for the example store in the Shopify Admin (see Figure 4-5) and in the header.liquid section (see Listing 4-5), with the result on the frontend (see Figure 4-6).

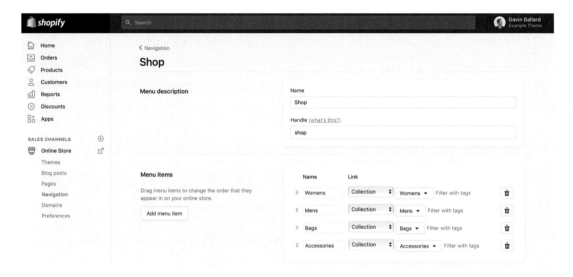

***Figure 4-5.*** *Configuration of a sub-navigation menu in the Shopify Admin*

***Listing 4-5.*** The Navigation Menu Link Loop Updated to Handle Submenu
Navigation Items

```
{%- for link in primary_link_list.links -%}
  {%- assign child_link_list_handle = link.title | handle -%}
  {%- assign child_link_list = linklists[child_link_list_handle] -%}
  {%- if child_link_list and child_link_list.links.size > 0 -%}
    {%- assign has_child_link_list = true %}
  {%- else- %}
    {%- assign has_child_link_list = false %}
  {%- endif -%}

  <li>
    <a href="{{ link.url }}">
      {{ link.title | escape }}
    </a>
    {%- if has_child_link_list -%}
      <div class="dropdown-menu">
        {%- for child_link in child_link_list.links -%}
          <a href="{{ child_link.url }}">{{ child_link.title | escape }}</a>
        {%- endfor -%}
      </div>
```

```
    {%- endif -%}
  </li>
{%- endfor -%}
```

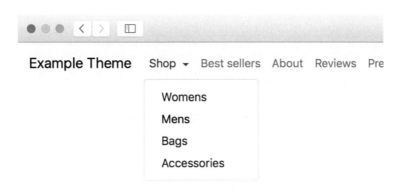

***Figure 4-6.***  *The resulting simple dropdown menu on the Example Theme storefront*

Some design guidelines when implementing dropdown menus:

- Try to avoid any menus with more than seven options, as this begins to create too much mental overhead for users. If you feel you need more than this, consider adding another level of hierarchy or just relying on a smooth filtering experience on collection pages to let users narrow down their results. Remember that this is a limit, not a goal—ASOS has only three top-level menu items on their store (Home, Men, and Women).

- Keep dropdowns to a single level. Although it's tempting to add submenus on the side of a dropdown, research shows they're fiddly and tricky for users. This is especially true when dropdowns are hover-activated—users "lose" the menu unless they are very careful with the mouse. If you need to be able to display a larger category range, consider a mega-menu, discussed in the next section.

- Activate dropdowns via a click, not a hover. This means you don't have
  to worry about a difference experience for touch devices like mobile
  and tablet (where you don't get a hover event). It also allows you to keep
  an opened menu in place even if the cursor leaves the menu, avoiding a
  major source of frustration for users and potential accessibility issues.

The dropdown menu in Figure 4-7 is an example of a menu with a number of
problems. First, it's far too long, meaning customers have to scroll just to see all the
options. Second, it's hover-activated and closes instantly when the mouse leaves it (very
common when scrolling to see the bottom). Finally, it has submenus that suffer from
the same hover problems and that aren't hinted at by the main menu (by a right-angled
chevron, for example).

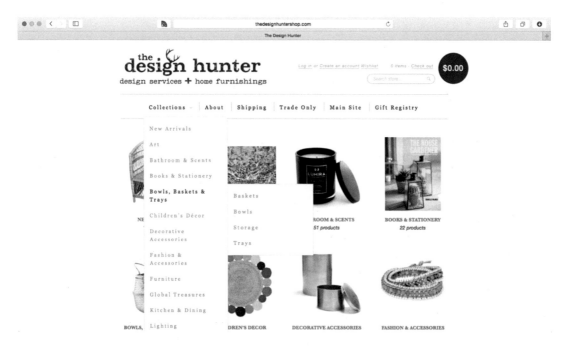

***Figure 4-7.*** *A dropdown menu with a number of usability problems*

## Mega-Menus

If you have a lot of categories, you might find you have too much information to fit into a
single level of dropdowns. That's where the common mega-menu design pattern comes
in to play. Mega-menus let you offer many deep navigation choices to users, presented in
a structure you can control and illustrate if needed (see Figure 4-8).

**Figure 4-8.** *While quite cluttered, this example shows how mega-menus can be used to categorize a large number of deep links on the ASOS site*

Because mega-menus offer a high degree of space and flexibility, they should be treated as a design canvas unto themselves rather than just a way to list a bunch of items. Doing this, in combination with the following recommendations, will help you make the most of your menus and provide a better shopping experience to customers.

- Use headings and columns to clearly break down and identify the chosen sections of your menu. The choice of columns should reflect the common ways customers may want to browse the product range—e.g., Shop by Size, Shop by Brand, and Shop by Price.

- You don't need to simply order products or categories alphabetically. Use the flexibility of the mega-menu to promote your best selling or featured items on the top left of the menu.

- Keep mega-menus short. Making menus too tall presents problems for users with small screens. You can compensate by using the full width of the screen.

- Don't be afraid to use images or graphics to enhance products or categories (without going overboard and turning your mega-menu into a visual mess).

- Ensure your menus are mobile friendly by using responsive design techniques.

The Sunglass Hut has an excellent example of an effective mega-menu, shown in Figure 4-9. A considered selection of top-level items (Hers, His…) opens (with a click!) a mega-menu that offers further deep navigation. The menu effectively makes use of graphics to offer a Featured Brands functionality as well as a featured collection at the bottom.

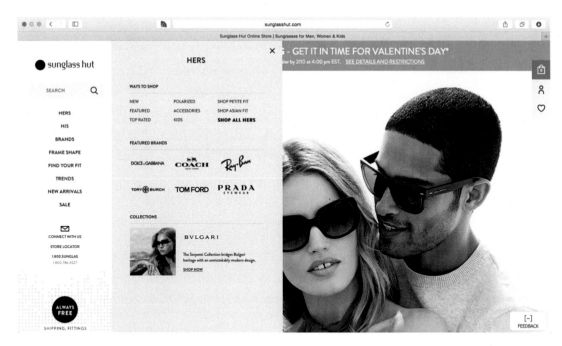

**Figure 4-9.**  *The Sunglass Hut's interesting horizontal twist on the mega-menu is a great example of menu design*

The implementation logic behind a mega-menu is similar to the existing dropdown menu we've implemented on the example theme; the key difference is in the styling and sizing of the elements displayed. For this reason, and because we're not yet dealing with that many products, let's leave the implementation of a mega-menu on the store for now and move on to another important navigation element—the footer.

## The Site Footer

More than just a spot to dump an e-mail signup form, designers often overlook the incredibly useful role footers play in navigation. They can serve as a get out of jail tool for users who have made it to the bottom of the page without finding what they're looking for, reducing the chance of someone bouncing off your site. Thanks to convention, they are also often the first place customers will look when in search of your shipping, refund, and return policies.

Additionally, footers are a great place to place trust signals like "secure" or "trusted" site badges and logos, logos of well-known customers, or logos of media companies that have covered your brand. Studies show that reinforcing the trustworthiness of your site with these types of signals on every page can have a positive impact on conversion rates.

---

**Note**    All this useful information in the footer can be lost if your store implements "infinite scroll" techniques on collection pages. This is one of a couple of reasons I don't recommend using infinite scroll on Ecommerce sites. You'll dig into this more in Chapter 6 when diving into collection page design.

---

To implement a footer in the example theme, we're going to take a similar approach to the header and create a new section called `footer.liquid` (see Listing 4-6) then include it from `theme.liquid` (see Listing 4-7), this time underneath the `{{ content_for_layout }}` tag. Like with `sections/header.liquid`, we need to include a `{% schema %}` section at the top to allow users to customize the footer.

*Listing 4-6.* The Contents of the New sections/footer.liquid File

```liquid
{% schema %}
{
  "name": "Footer",
  "blocks": [
    {
      "type": "link_list",
      "name": "Navigation menu",
      "settings": [
        {
          "id": "link_list",
          "type": "link_list",
          "label": "Navigation menu"
        }
      ]
    },
    {
      "type": "payment_icons",
      "name": "Payment icons"
    }
  ]
}
{% endschema %}
<footer>
  {%- for block in section.blocks -%}
    {%- case block.type -%}
      {%- when 'link_list' -%}
        {%- include 'footer-block-link-list' -%}
      {%- when 'payment_icons' -%}
        {%- include 'footer-block-payment-icons' -%}
    {%- endcase -%}
  {%- endfor -%}
</footer>
```

***Listing 4-7.*** The Inclusion of the New Footer Section in theme.liquid

```
...
{{ content_for_layout }}
{%- section 'footer' -%}
{{- 'jquery-3.1.1.min.js' | asset_url | script_tag -}}
...
```

The footer.liquid code introduces a new Liquid concept: *blocks*. Blocks are wrappers around content and settings, which can be added, removed, and reordered within a particular section. It makes sense to use blocks when you'd like to allow the theme owner to define repeated sections of content, or control the order content appears in.

In this footer, we defined two type of blocks within the footer section—a link_list type and a payment_icons type. The first allows the rendering of a vertical navigation menu within a footer column, the second displays a list of supported payment icons on the storefront. From the theme customizer, storeowners will be able to add and remove these blocks to configure the footer at will.

In footer.liquid, the code loops over each block configured in the section, checks its type, and includes either footer-block-link-list.liquid or footer-block-payment-icons.liquid. These are Liquid snippet files, stored in the theme's snippets directory in order to logically partition and simplify the code in the footer.liquid section. The filenames used here are just a convention to identify that they are included as blocks from within the footer section). Check out the example theme repository for the full implementation of these snippets.

Figure 4-10 shows the result of adding the footer in the theme customizer and in the theme preview.

***Figure 4-10.*** *Adding the footer snippet gives a customizable multi-column footer layout*

> **EXERCISE: LAYOUT AND NAVIGATION**
>
> 1. Following the steps from this chapter, add header and footer sections to your theme, including the configurable {% schema %} sections to allow users to configure the navigation menus to be used in each section.
>
> 2. Design an information hierarchy for the most important pages for your own hypothetical store, including a product hierarchy and sensible categorization system.
>
> 3. If your information hierarchy calls for multiple levels of information, add a dropdown menu to your main navigation to make it easier for customers to find what they're looking for. If you're feeling plucky, implement the dropdown menu as a mega-menu with some additional graphical information inside the expanded area.

# Summary

In this chapter, we've set ourselves up nicely for building a new Shopify theme. The chapter covered the options and frameworks that developers have access to when starting a new theme, and explained how we can use preexisting sample product CSVs to start building around realistic data.

You learned about some key Shopify concepts like layouts, sections, and blocks, and read about the design principles to apply when laying out the navigation for a store's theme.

# CHAPTER 5

# Designing Product Pages

Once we have a basic theme structure to work with, we can start to build out the individual pages on the store. This chapter starts with the most important one—the product page.

## The Product Page

The product page is usually the most important page for an Ecommerce store. It's where a customer evaluates an offering and makes the crucial decision to purchase. It needs to convey a lot of information to visitors—core information like what your product is, does, and looks like; how much it costs; what configuration options are available; and supplementary information like size guides, shipping details, product guides, and customer reviews.

In addition to presenting all this information clearly, it needs to provide interactive elements to help customers configure the product to their liking (e.g., selecting the appropriate size and color), add it to the cart, and progress to the checkout.

In my experience, both designers and storeowners spend too much time thinking about and refining the home page of a site, at the expense of the product page. It's totally understandable—the home page is what the storeowner types in when they want to look at their site, after all—but it's easy to overlook the fact that many visitors to a store don't land on the home page and progress linearly from there to the collection page and product page. Figure 5-1 shows how designers and storeowners often conceptualize the customer journeys through their site (left) versus the reality (right). If you're designing a theme for an existing store, you can ask for access to any existing analytics data in order to understand the most common paths for the merchant's actual customers.

© Gavin Ballard 2017
G. Ballard, *The Definitive Guide to Shopify Themes*, DOI 10.1007/978-1-4842-2641-4_5

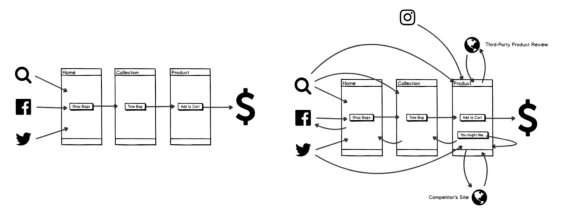

**Figure 5-1.** *How designers and storeowners visualize the customer journey through their sites (left) versus the reality (right)*

Customers arriving on a site from a Google search, paid advertisement, or social network are more likely to be landing directly on a specific product page that matches their interest instead of the home page, so it's crucial to make sure that the experience on that page is as smooth as possible.

For this reason, I encourage you to start design and development work on the product page first, which is what we're going to do with the example theme in this chapter.

# Product Page Information Hierarchy

To design an effective product page, we first need to establish the *information hierarchy*—which bits of product information are most important to our visitors? What should we prioritize, and what can be considered as "supplemental" information that doesn't need to be as prominent?

The answers will differ from store to store, although there tends to be some information that's usually more important than others. A "standard" information hierarchy, placing product information into prioritized buckets, might look like Figure 5-2.

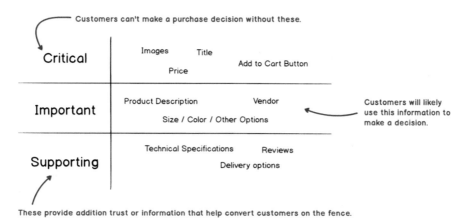

**Figure 5-2.** *A "standard" product information hierarchy*

Deviations from this standard hierarchy might occur because of the types of products we're selling, what we know about the customers visiting the stores, or even what devices we anticipate visitors using. As an example, compare the product page for Colonna Coffee's roasted coffee beans with the product page for Bespoke Verse's gift mug in Figure 5-3. Colonna's coffee bean packaging looks similar regardless of the roast or flavor profile, so the product image is relatively small, with emphasis placed on the textual description of the coffee's taste and its available options (espresso versus filter, long versus short). Conversely, Bespoke Verse's gift mug doesn't need any description at all, as the product image does all the talking and is placed very prominently.

**Figure 5-3.** *The product pages for whole coffee beans on Colonna Coffee (colonnacoffee.com, left) and a gift mug on Bespoke Verse (www.bespokeverse. co.uk, right)*

For this example theme, we'll be working with the "standard" information hierarchy from Figure 5-2. The first pass will use a layout based on the rough mockups in Figure 5-4 to achieve this. As you can see, I've applied the hierarchy independently for both mobile and desktop contexts, to make sure that I am prioritizing information consistently but also considering how users will experience the page on different devices.

*Figure 5-4.*  *Rough mockups for the example theme's product page, based on the standard product information hierarchy and inserted into the layout format developed in Chapter 4*

# Adding Product Imagery

Let's get started with the code implementation of the product page in the example theme.

By default, all products on the store are displayed using `templates/product.liquid`. As with other page template files, the contents of `product.liquid` are processed by Shopify and rendered inside the `{{ content_for_layout }}` tag of `theme.liquid`. We're going to start adding content to `product.liquid` with the code for a simple product image carousel. A simplified version of the HTML code for this is found in Listing 5-1, with the result displayed in Figure 5-5. If the product has more than one image, a list of product image thumbnails is shown. The more detailed product.liquid used to generate the product template shown in Figure 5-5 is available in the example theme GitHub repository.

***Listing 5-1.*** A Simplified Version of a product.liquid Displaying a Main Product

```
<main>
    <div id="column-left">
      {%- if product.images.size > 0 -%}
        <img src="{{ image | product_img_url: '480x480', scale: 2, crop:
        'center' }}" alt="{{ product.title | escape }}" />

        {%- if product.images.size > 0 -%}
        <ul id="thumbnails">
          {%- for image in product.images -%}
            <li>
              <a href="{{ image | product_img_url: 'master' }}" target="_
              blank">
                <img src="{{ image | product_img_url: '240x240', scale: 2,
                crop: 'center' }}" alt="{{ product.title | escape }}" />
              </a>
            </li>
          {%- endfor -%}
        </ul>
        {%- endif -%}
      {%- else -%}
        {{ 'image' | placeholder_svg_tag }}
      {%- endif -%}
    </div>
</main>
```

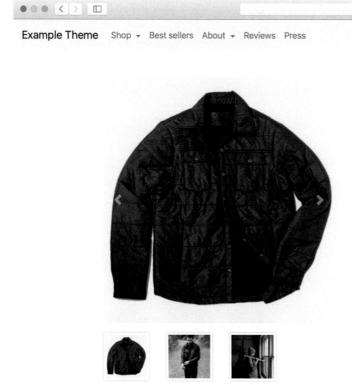

**Figure 5-5.** *The result of Listing 5-1 on an example product page*

Here, I've added some HTML markup for a left column to insert the product images into. Using Liquid, we query the `product` variable (made available automatically by Shopify on all product pages) to see if any images have been added to the product by the storeowner (`{%- if product.images.size > 0 -%}`). If so, we display the "primary" image in a large `<img>` tag, and, if the product has more than one image, we iterate over all product images to generate a list of product thumbnails.

For now, the implementation opens images in a new browser window when the thumbnail images are clicked, rather than swapping out the large product image for the thumbnail version. If you check the more extensive example in the GitHub repository, you'll see that I've leveraged a carousel control that allows the users to slide through product images with left/right controls, as well as skip to a specific product image using the thumbnails.

# Design Considerations for Product Images

While we're in the process of adding product images to your example theme, it's worth considering some high-level design guidelines. Product imagery should generally:

- Be large (easy to discern details, even on smaller screens and for visitors with poor eyesight)

- Be of high quality (both in terms of production technique and the file quality)

- For physical products, give a sense of the scale of the product

- Display the product both by itself and in use

- Not use any overt filters or digital alteration

- Be as consistent as possible in terms of look, feel, and aspect ratio

You won't always have control over the product imagery used in your themes, but when you do, try to advocate for these principles. Encourage clients to invest time and budget on professionally-shot imagery (ideally, by a studio with specific experience in Ecommerce product photography). Customers are very sensitive to the quality of product photography on an Ecommerce site and will be much less likely to convert if your product images look unprofessional.

One of the best things you can do at the start of a theme design project is set firm guidelines on product image resolution and aspect ratio. Request that merchants upload images in the highest resolution possible (2048 x 2048 pixels is a good goal and the largest Shopify will render). To avoid bloating your page load times, you can make use of Shopify's image filters (discussed in the next section) to render a lower-resolution version of images where appropriate.

Sticking to one consistent aspect ratio for product images across the entire site reduces the likelihood of irregular or jarring differences in the appearance of products when they are rendered next to each other. I like to encourage square (1:1) images where possible, although 4:3 or 3:4 can work well depending on the types of products being sold. While you can use stylesheets and Shopify's image filters to crop, stretch, and trim images, it's always easier to do that with a common starting point.

# Shopify's Image Filters

One of Shopify's handy features is the ability to use Liquid filters to perform on-the-fly image resizing and manipulation. This means that storeowners can upload the highest-resolution version of a product image to the backend, and a theme developer can use these filters to generate a version that's the appropriate size and aspect ratio for a given location.

The key filter in question is called `product_img_url`, and you can see it being used in Listing 5-1. You can check the Shopify documentation for the details,[1] but key uses for the filter include:

- Using smaller versions of an image to decrease file size and page load times (you'll be learning about this in Chapter 10 on performance)

- Cropping or padding images to ensure they have a consistent aspect ratio

- Converting images to Progressive JPEGs for faster load times

# Zoomable Product Images and Product Lightboxes

Implementing zooming product images (where mousing over a product image provides a "zoomed" version of it), or product lightboxes (where clicking a product image pops open a "modal" full-screen product image) can be a great way of letting customers get up close with your productions, but it's critical that these design elements don't break the users' flow by making them feel like they've left the original product page. Other things to be wary of when implementing these features are:

- They should be *progressively enhanced*, maintaining usability if JavaScript isn't available.

- Consider disabling them on mobile devices, where product images will often be full width already, or where users are used to pinching a touch device to zoom in on images.

- Ensure that they are keyboard accessible in that users should be able to move through successive images using their arrow keys and close the lightbox with the Escape key.

---

[1]https://help.shopify.com/themes/liquid/filters/url-filters#product_img_url.

# Product Video

Adding relevant video to a product page can result in some dramatic conversion improvements[2] and it's likely that more and more online retailers will make use of video to better demonstrate their products and unique selling proposition.

How you incorporate video into your theme will depend on whether high-quality video will be available for all products, or just a limited subset. If a large, high-quality video is available for every product on the store, then setting aside a prominent amount of space for those videos on every product page makes sense, as demonstrated on the Sonos site in Figure 5-6.

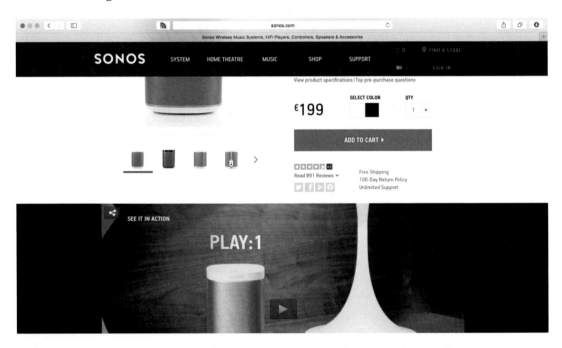

***Figure 5-6.***  *Sonos makes product video very prominent on its product pages*

Themes for stores that either don't have videos for all products or have multiple videos for each product can display these through a second Thumbnails section.

Avoid using embedded video tools that automatically load and present controls or branding (such as YouTube), as they can be distracting for the user. In fact, for performance reasons, it's best to avoid loading a JavaScript-heavy player at all on page

---

[2]See, for example, `https://blog.kissmetrics.com/product-videos-conversion/`.

load, and instead provide an image that triggers a video player popup or embed when the user clicks on it. See Figure 5-7.

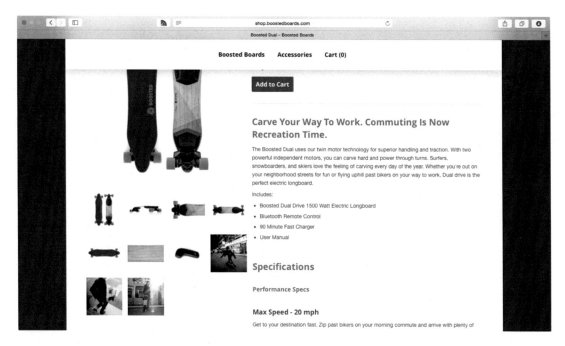

***Figure 5-7.*** *Boosted Boards does a good job of showing off their products, but some of their product thumbnails are videos. They could improve discoverability of this by adding a "Play Video" overlay to these thumbnails*

# Adding Product Details and the Add To Cart Form

Jumping back to the example theme, we're now going to flesh out the content on the right side of the desktop mockups from Figure 5-4: the product's details, description, and a basic Add To Cart form. Listing 5-2 shows a simplified version of the Liquid code we need to achieve this, with Figure 5-8 displaying the result in the browser.

***Listing 5-2.*** Additions to templates/product.liquid to Add Product Information and Add To Cart Form

```
<main>
  ... (product image code omitted) ...
  <div id="column-right">
    <h1>{{ product.title | escape }}</h1>
    <h5>{{ product.vendor | escape }}</h5>
```

```
    <h3>{% if product.price_varies %}{{ product.price_min | money }}
    - {{ product.price_max | money }}{% else %}{{ product.price | money }}
    {% endif %}
h3>

    {{ product.description }}

    <form action="/cart/add" method="post" role="form">

      {%- if product.variants.size > 1 -%}
        <label for="product-select">Select your {{ product.title |
        downcase }}</label>
        <select id="product-select" name="id">
          {%- for variant in product.variants -%}
            <option {% if variant == product.selected_or_first_available_
            variant %} selected="selected" {% endif %} value=
            "{{ variant.id }}">{{ variant.title | escape }} -
            {{ variant.price | money }}</option>
          {%- endfor -%}
        </select>
      {%- else -%}
        <input type="hidden" name="id" value="{{ product.variants.
        first.id }}" />
      {%- endif -%}

      <button type="submit" {% unless product.available %}
      disabled="disabled"{% endunless %}>Add to cart</button>

    </form>
  </div>
</main>
```

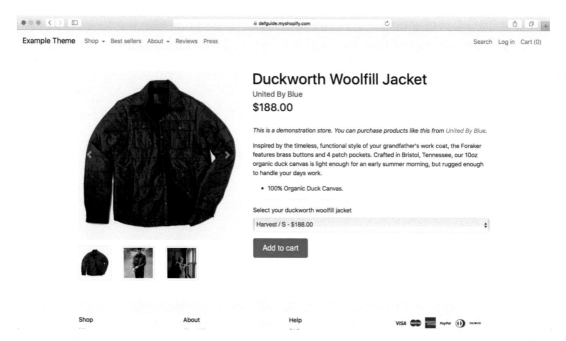

***Figure 5-8.*** *The example product page, with product information and the Add To Cart form added*

Let's break down these changes.

# Product Details and Description

There's nothing too involved with the code in Listing 5-2 used to render the product details and description. It's really just a matter of outputting the appropriate Liquid variable (`product.title`, `product.min_price`) in a HTML element like an `<h1>` that gives the appropriate information hierarchy.

I've used a couple of Liquid filters to output this information. I use the | `escape` filter when outputting the title and vendor. This is a good practice to follow when outputting any user-generated text content, to avoid any potential formatting or output issues (for example, if your product title contains a HTML character like <, the escape filter will ensure it's rendered as text and not as HTML). I'm also using the | `money` filter to display the price of the product (stored by Shopify as cents, e.g. **18800**) in a format determined by the store's currency and preferences.

The `product.description` is output directly. It can contain HTML (to allow for things like anchor links inside the description content), so we don't use the | `escape` filter on it. If you want to guarantee that the description doesn't render anything

funky that could break your page layout, you can force it to text only using the
`| strip_html` filter.

You may have noticed the example uses some Liquid logic when displaying the
price of the product. This is done because it's possible for different product variants
(combinations of colors and sizes, for example) to have different prices. We should check
if that's the case for this product (`{% if product.price_varies %}`) to decide whether
to display a single price (`product.price`) or the price range (`product.price_min` to
`product.price_max`). Later in this chapter, you'll see how you can tweak this approach to
dynamically update the `price` element to display only the price of the currently selected
variant.

---

**Tip**   Use real product descriptions rather than dummy or placeholder (lorem
ipsum) text when designing your product pages. You'll get a much better sense of
how the product will look and flow and avoid surprises down the road.

Another thing to avoid is copying and pasting product descriptions from
manufacturer or competitor sites. Not only are there potentially negative SEO
consequences for duplicating content in this way, you miss the opportunity to
insert your brand's unique voice into the description and persuade customers.

---

# Add To Cart Form

In its most simple form, a Shopify Add To Cart form is a `<form>` element that uses the
POST method to submit to the `/cart/add` URL on the storefront. The only piece of
information that's required to be submitted in the form's data is the ID of one or more
variants to add to the cart (these parameters should be named `id` if adding a single
variant or `id[]` if adding multiple variants at once).

In this example, we allow the customer to select which variant to add to the cart
using a `<select>` dropdown element, which contains a list of all the product's variants
and displays a description of them alongside their price. Before rendering the dropdown,
we check that it's actually needed (`{% if product.variants.size > 1 %}`). If there's
only one variant, we just provide its ID as a parameter to the form using a hidden input.

When rendering the available options in the select dropdown, we use a Liquid
variable called `product.selected_or_first_available_variant` to see whether we
should make a particular option selected by default when loading the page. `product.
selected_or_first_available_variant` is a verbose but accurately named variable

used with either the "selected" variant (determined by a ?variant = parameter in the request URL) **or** the first "available" product variant, where availability is determined by a variant being in stock based on the merchant's inventory policies. See Figure 5-9.

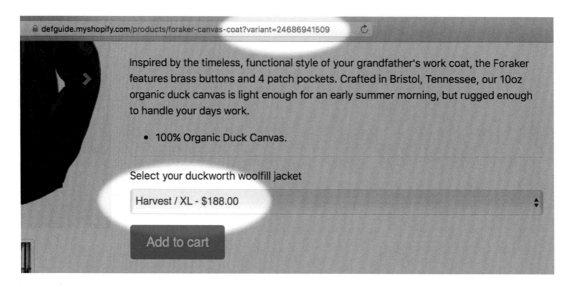

***Figure 5-9.*** *Specifying a variant ID in the ?variant= parameter in the URL preselects that variant in the Add To Cart form's dropdown*

The final element of the Add To Cart form is the all-important Submit button. In this example, this is implemented as a standard HTML button. I've added a bit of Liquid logic to disable the Add button if the product isn't available (meaning all variants are sold out).

This initial Add To Cart form is simple, but it's an important foundation that we can build on to add support for more dynamic variant selectors, custom inputs, and Ajax functionality. As we add these extras, it's important to keep fundamental usability and accessibility guidelines in mind, by:

- Ensuring all inputs have associated labels

- Trying to avoid inline form elements and inputs

- Using appropriate HTML5 input types (e.g., type="number")

- Making sensible choices for input type (e.g., using radio inputs rather than select dropdowns for options with few choices)

- Keeping all inputs keyboard-accessible

- Ensuring action inputs like Submit buttons are clearly indicated and give the appearance of being interactive

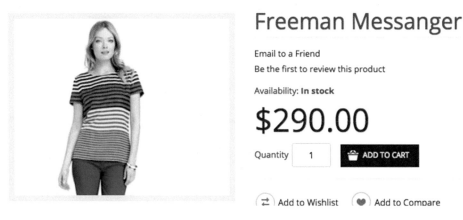

**Figure 5-10.**  *This Add To Cart button's size and flat appearance makes it look like a label, rather than an interactive button that encourages clicking*

# Adding Recommended Products

We're nearly done implementing our planned layout from Figure 5-4, with only the addition of the "You may also like..." recommended products section at the bottom of the page.

# Related versus Alternate Products

Many themes get confused or don't draw a distinction between two different types of recommended products: related products and alternate products.

- *Related products* are accessories or complements to the currently visible product. Think compatible batteries for a camera, or a matching scarf for a cardigan. Displaying a list of related products on a product page both provides an "upsell" path to encourage additional customer purchases. It also increases a customer's awareness of the store's overall product range.

- *Alternate products*, as the name suggests, are a possible substitute or alternative for the currently visible product. Think an Xbox instead of a PlayStation, or an overcoat in an alternative style. Unlike related products, the purpose of a list of alternate products isn't to increase the size of a customer's cart, but rather to make sure that they can find what they're looking for in the first place.

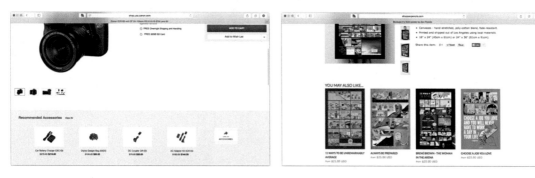

***Figure 5-11.*** *The Recommended Accessories section on the Canon site is a good example of upselling through related products (left). Zen Pencil's "You May Also Like..." section suggests alternative posters as a substitute to the current selection (right)*

Because related and alternate products serve two very different purposes, they shouldn't be displayed together. They should be clearly labeled, so that customers can understand the source of their recommendation—using language like "Users Who Bought This Also Bought..." instead of "Related Products" and "We Think You May Also Like..." instead of "Alternate Products".

Adding a small Ajax-powered Add To Cart link next to related products is a good way to make these upsells painless for the customer without taking them away from the main product page.

# Recommended Products on Shopify

Shopify doesn't provide any explicit built-in support for managing lists of recommended products, although there are many Shopify Apps that offer this functionality (search for "product recommendations" in the Shopify App Store).

While these apps can do some pretty nifty things, like using sales data to algorithmically generate recommendations, or tailoring recommendations to individual visitors, I prefer to try tackling problems with Shopify's "native" concepts and some custom Liquid code before resorting to an app. Not only does this lower the ongoing costs involved in running a store, it reduces the risk of apps interfering with each other and breaking store functionality or negatively impacting on performance. While apps might offer slightly more functionality, in many cases a theme-based solution will be more than good enough for a merchant's needs.

There are a couple of ways we can use built-in Shopify features to elegantly implement related and alternate product functionality. First, we can allow a storeowner to manually specify a list of recommended products for each product on their stores, then display that list in the product template. This specification can be achieved by the storeowner using one of two methods:

- By setting a *metafield* on the product containing a list of related product handles. You'll learn more about metafields later in this chapter; for now, all you need to know is that they allow storeowners to store custom information on products and other Shopify objects. This information can be retrieved in Liquid and used to render a list of related products.

- By using a *naming convention* where a collection is created with a URL (handle) that matches the product, and then populating that collection with the desired related products. For example, if the product's handle is `foraker-canvas-coat`, the storeowner can create a collection with the handle `foraker-canvas-coat-related`. The Liquid code can calculate the expected name of the relevant related products collection for the current product, check if it exists, and display the products if so.

Specifying recommended products manually has the advantage of giving storeowners fine-grained control over the products that appear in a products list, but it has the disadvantage of being time consuming to create and maintain. As an alternative, we can use some Liquid logic to automatically calculate a list of related products. Again, we have two possible strategies:

- Find a non-generic collection the current product is a member of and consider the other products in that collection to be "related." This can be a naïve approach, but often produces results good enough for many use cases.

- Compare the current product to all other products on the store and "score" them based on the number of tags and collections they share with the current product. Products with a higher score are considered closely related to the current product. The implementation of this approach is a little more involved but it can yield better results than the first method.

For the example theme, we're going to implement a Liquid snippet (`snippets/related-products.liquid` in the theme's directory) that supports three of these approaches to display a list of up to four related products on the page. When included on the product page, it will:

1. Check if the product has a "related products" metafield defined. If so, it will use that to render the first four products listed in that metafield.

2. If no "related products" metafield is defined, then it will check to see if a collection with the same handle as the product (but with `-related` on the end) exists. If so, it will render the first four products in that collection.

3. If neither a metafield or a collection exists, then it will fall back to finding a collection the current product is member of and render the first four products in that collection.

This approach gives us a basic way of automatically finding related products on every product page, while giving the storeowner the option of creating a collection or metafield to override the default behavior if they need more control. An outline of the the snippet's logic is given in Listing 5-3 (it's truncated for brevity; the full version is available in the example theme repository). Listing 5-4 shows how to include the snippet inside `product.liquid`. Finally, Figure 5-11 shows the result of implementation in the browser.

***Listing 5-3.*** The Logic Outline for a related-products.liquid Liquid Snippet

```
{%- assign RELATED_PRODUCTS_LIMIT = 4 -%}
{%- if product.metafields.theme.related_products != blank -%}

  {%- assign related_product_handles = product.metafields.theme.related_
  products | split: ',' -%}
  {%- for related_product_handle in related_product_handles -%}
    ... render products from metafield...
  {%- endfor -%}
{%- else -%}

  {%- assign related_collection_handle = product.handle | append:
  '-related' -%}
  {%- assign related_collection = collections[related_collection_handle] -%}
```

```
{%- if related_collection and related_collection.products.size > 0 %}
  {%- for related_product in related_collection.products limit:
  RELATED_PRODUCTS_LIMIT -%}
    ... render products from collection...
  {%- endfor -%}
{%- else -%}

  {%- assign related_collection = nil -%}
  {%- for collection in product.collections -%}
    {%- unless collection.handle == 'all' -%}
    {%- if related_collection == blank or collection.products.size >
    related_collection.products.size -%}
      {%- assign related_collection = collection -%}
      {%- if related_collection.products.size > 5 -%}
        {%- break -%}
      {%- endif -%}
    {%- endif -%}
    {%- endunless -%}
  {%- endfor -%}

  {%- for related_product in related_collection.products limit:
  RELATED_PRODUCTS_LIMIT -%}
    ... render products from collection...
  {%- endfor -%}

  {%- endif -%}
{%- endif -%}
```

***Listing 5-4.*** Inclusion of Related Products Liquid Snippet at the Bottom of
templates/product.liquid

```
<main>

  <div id="column-left">
    ...
  </div>
```

```
<div id="column-right">
   ...
</div>
<h3>You may also like</h3>
{%- include 'related-products' -%}

</main>
```

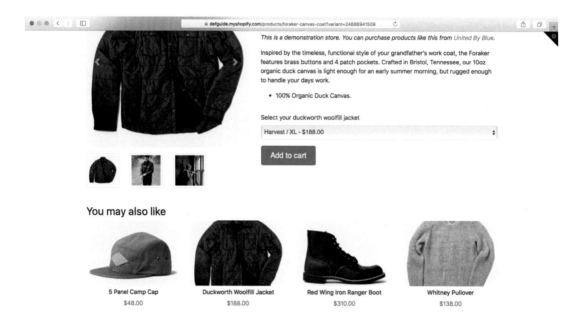

***Figure 5-12.***  *The result of adding the related product snippet at the bottom of the example theme's product page*

# Improving the Product Page

Congratulations! The desktop version of your product page has now fully implemented your planned layout design from Figure 5-4. You have a simple, but fully-functional, product page that customers can use to view your products, select a desired product variant, and add that selection to their carts. Because this page is so simple, it's very quick to load and doesn't require any JavaScript to function.

For the rest of this chapter, we'll be walking through the implementation of common features that theme designers might add to this starting point.

# Adding Product Information

In the original product information hierarchy (see Figure 5-2), we identified a "supporting" class of information—product details not as crucial as title or price but which are still likely be used by customers to help them make a purchasing decision. Common examples of this would be a product's technical specifications, shipping and returns information, size guides, or garment care information. When adding this sort of information to a product page, we need to consider:

- How best to display the information (as a table, graphic, chart, text, etc.)

- How prominent to make the information on the page, and where to place it (inline further down the page, inside a tab component, in a popup dialog, etc.)

- Whether the information is relevant to every product on the store, or only a subset

- Whether the information varies from product to product, or if it's consistent across the store

- Where to store the additional product information, and how to give storeowners the ability to manage and update that information

For the purposes of the example theme, we're going to implement a common pattern for additional production information—turning the production description section into a tabbed panel that allows customers to view shipping information in a separate tab. We'll also allow the storeowner to use Shopify metafields to specify garment care information on a per-product basis and display that information in a separate tab where present.

Listing 5-5 shows a simple implementation of the tabs in question, extracted out into a `product-details.liquid` snippet and displaying the dynamic product description in one tab and some static shipping information in the other. Figure 5-13 shows the result.

***Listing 5-5.*** Simple Implementation of Some Product Information Tabs

```
<ul role="tablist">
  <li>
    <a href="#description" role="tab">Description</a>
  </li>
```

```
<li>
  <a href="#shipping" role="tab">Shipping</a>
</li>
</ul>

<div class="tab-content">
  <div id="description" role="tabpanel" class="active">
      {{ product.description }}
  </div>
  <div role="tabpanel" class="tab-pane" id="shipping">
    <p>
      Orders placed before 4pm are shipped the same day.
      The table below shows approximate shipping times using our standard
      shipping service.
    </p>
    <table>
      ...
    </table>
  </div>
</div>
```

**Duckworth Woolfill Jacket**
United By Blue
**$188.00**

| Description | Shipping |
| --- | --- |

*This is a demonstration store. You can purchase products like this from United By Blue.*

Inspired by the timeless, functional style of your grandfather's work coat, the Foraker features brass buttons and 4 patch pockets. Crafted in Bristol, Tennessee, our 10oz organic duck canvas is light enough for an early summer morning, but rugged enough to handle your days work.

- 100% Organic Duck Canvas.

Select your duckworth woolfill jacket

Harvest / XL - $188.00 ▾

Add to cart

**Duckworth Woolfill Jacket**
United By Blue
**$188.00**

| Description | Shipping |
| --- | --- |

Orders placed before 4pm are shipped the same day. The table below shows approximate shipping times using our standard shipping service.

| Eastern states | 2-3 business days |
| --- | --- |
| Australia and New Zealand | 3-4 business days |
| International | 7-10 business days |

Select your duckworth woolfill jacket

Harvest / XL - $188.00 ▾

Add to cart

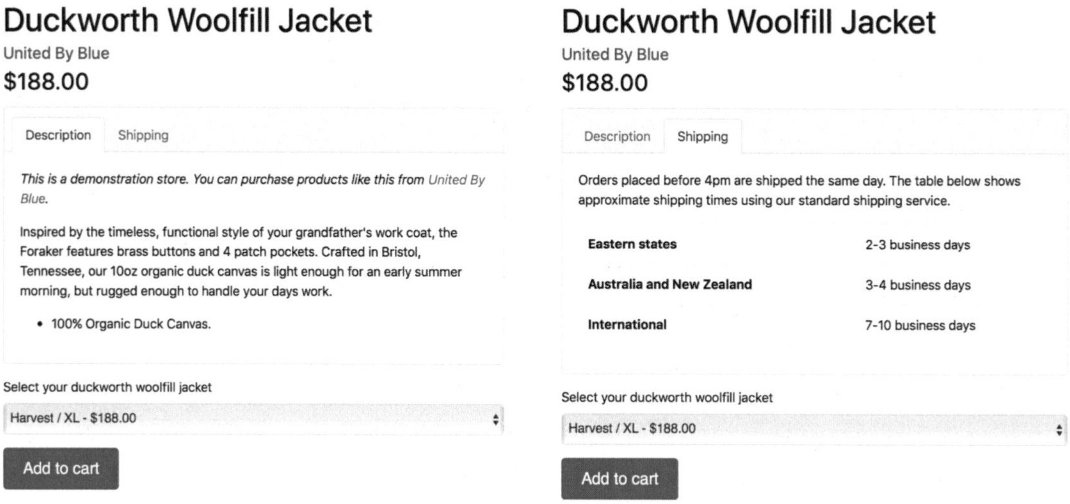

***Figure 5-13.*** *The addition of the product description tabs from Listing 5-5 to the product details screen*

## Managing Additional Information with Metafields

The next step is to add a Garment Care tab to the product page. We can't just statically code this tab in as we did with the Shipping Information tab, as the content of the tab—and whether the tab is displayed at all—will differ from product to product.

One potential solution is to code the care information directly into the Liquid templates—something like Listing 5-6.

***Listing 5-6.*** A Possible (But Not Recommended) Approach to Conditionally Displaying Garment Care Information

```
<ul role="tablist">
  ...
  {%- if product.handle == 'foraker-canvas-coat' -%}
  <li>
    <a href="#garment-care" role="tab">Garment Care</a>
  </li>
  {%- endif -%}
  ...
</ul>

<div class="tab-content">
  ...
  {%- if product.handle == 'foraker-canvas-coat' -%}
  <div role="tabpanel" class="tab-pane" id="garment-care">
      <p>
    Always store in a dry, well-ventilated area.
      </p>
  </div>
  {%- endif -%}
  ...
</div>
```

The limitation of this approach is that it requires us to open the Liquid template and make changes any time we want to make alterations to the garment care information itself or add care information to a new product. In general, managing content inside Liquid templates is a recipe for disaster. It's unwieldy for storeowners to manage and is prone to being overwritten by other users or automated theme deployment scripts.

It also means that an inexperienced storeowner can forget to close a HTML tag and wreak havoc with all the site's product pages.

We're going to get around this issue by using *metafields*, a feature of Shopify that allows the storage of arbitrary custom data against objects like products, customer, collections, and the like. Metafields are accessed in Liquid code like this: `{{ product.metafields.extra.garment_care }}`, where `extra` is a "namespace" or "group" for the metafields (designed to avoid metafield conflicts) and `garment_care` is the "key" for a specific metafield value.

Historically, Shopify made accessing and managing metafield data quite obtuse and didn't expose metafield controls on the product pages in the Shopify Admin, which is why there are dozens of Shopify apps that offer metafield functionality. However, you don't really need them—you're able to edit product metafields within the Shopify Admin by constructing a **bulk edit URL**, which looks like `https://defguide.myshopify.com/admin/bulk?resource_name=Product&edit=metafields.extra.garment_care:string`.[3]

If you open that URL in your browser (changing `defguide.myshopify.com` to match your own store domain), you'll be presented with a list of products and the ability to set a value for the `extra_garment` metafield key for each. Storeowners can bookmark this URL and return to it any time to update or add garment care information for one or more products.

With a strategy for managing care information in place, we can now update our product details snippet to conditionally display a Garment Care tab when the metafield is present and contains information, as in Listing 5-7. When implemented and the customer browses to a product that has garment care information set, we get the result in Figure 5-14. As mentioned, this improved version uses metafields, rather than hardcoded data, to display garment care information in a separate tab.

***Listing 5-7.*** Improved Version of Listing 5-6 that Uses Metafields

```
<ul role="tablist">
  ...
  {%- unless product.metafields.extra.garment_care == blank -%}
  <li>
```

---

[3]If you're a Google Chrome user, I highly recommend checking out ShopifyFD (`http://shopifyfd.com`), a Chrome extension that hooks into the Shopify Admin and allows the editing of metafields directly on product admin pages.

```
    <a href="#garment-care" role="tab">Garment Care</a>
  </li>
  {%- endunless -%}
  ...
</ul>

<div class="tab-content">
  ...
  {%- unless product.metafields.extra.garment_care == blank -%}
  <div role="tabpanel" class="tab-pane" id="garment-care">
      {{ product.metafields.extra.garment_care }}
  </div>
  {%- endunless -%}
  ...
</div>
```

## Duckworth Woolfill Jacket

United By Blue
**$188.00**

| Description | Garment Care | Shipping |

- Always store in a dry, well-ventilated area
- Do not place in a cupboard or plastic bag for long periods of time as it will become mouldy
- If your Oilskin garment has become mouldy, we recommend hanging it under full sun for a couple of weeks
- If garment is still mouldy, hand wash with pure soap and reproof

Select your duckworth woolfill jacket

| Harvest / XL - $188.00 | ▲▼ |

**Add to cart**

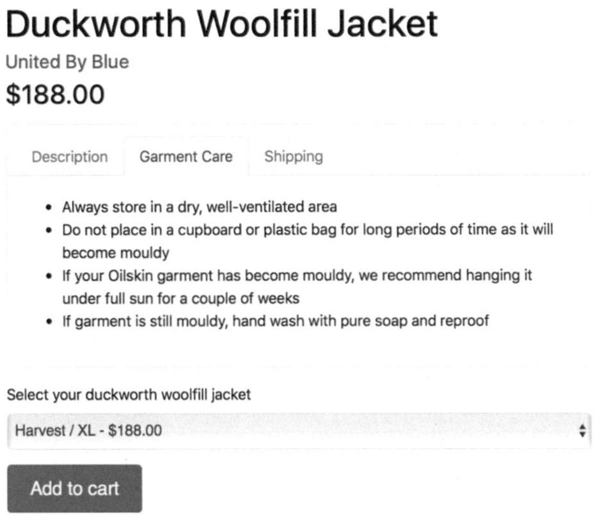

*Figure 5-14.* *The display of garment care information when the relevant metafield is present*

# Improving the Mobile Experience

Until now, the example has been focused on how the theme looks and works on the desktop. Doing this and ignoring the mobile experience—even if you're using a "responsive" framework—is dangerous in commerce. Over half of all traffic to Shopify stores is on mobile devices, and for some stores the numbers are as high as 75%.

As you're working on a Shopify theme, make sure you consider how customers browsing on a mobile device are going to view the information hierarchy or take key actions like adding products to the cart. This doesn't just mean resizing your browser on the desktop, either—you need to physically take out one or two devices and walk through the site to fully appreciate the different experience. Considerations like the size of touch areas, how hard the buttons are to reach with your thumb, and visible content areas all come in to play.

Take a look at Figure 5-15, which shows the state of the current example product page on a mobile. A couple of issues jump out:

- The initial view on the product page doesn't display the product title, vendor, or price—all information that we identified as important in our product hierarchy.

- The product image carousel displays the product image okay, but all the thumbnails are displayed beneath it as full width images, so we need to scroll a long way to get to the product information.

- The text on the Garment Care tab breaks to a new line and messes up the layout.

- Having the Add To Cart button less than half the width of the screen and over on the left makes it harder to reach with the thumb for a right-handed user holding a phone in one hand.

- Having only one product per row in the "You May Also Like…" section means it takes a long time to scroll through.

 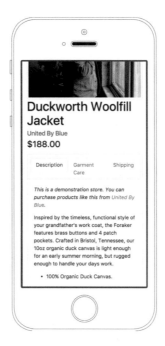 

***Figure 5-15.*** *Scrolling through the current product page on a mobile device, there are some display and usability issues that jump out*

Addressing these sorts of issues isn't usually hard, especially if you're using a CSS framework or library that provides responsive helper utilities. To resolve these issues in the example theme, I decided to:

- Add a version of the product title, vendor, and price to the top of the page that's only visible on mobile, and hide the same information lower down the page.

- Leave the product carousel with the expectation that mobile users can swipe left and right to browse the available product images, but hide the product thumbnails altogether.

- Hide the word Garment on the Garment Care tab on smaller screens, as Care conveys enough information. Another popular approach if you have more tabs is to swap to icons when you have less space to work with.

- Make the Add To Cart button full-width on mobile devices so that it's easier to reach.

- Display the related products in a 2x2 grid, rather than one per row.

The code implementing these changes is available in the example theme's repository. As you can see from Figure 5-16, they result in a much more usable mobile experience.

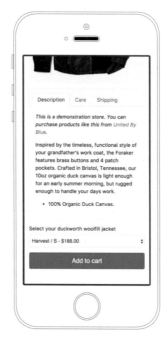
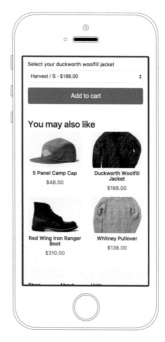

***Figure 5-16.*** *Just a few simple changes have addressed some of the major usability issues with the mobile version of the site*

# Creating Alternate Page Templates

The product page is looking pretty solid for now, so we're going to move on to some other areas of the site, starting with the home page in Chapter 6. Before we do that, I'm going to quickly cover one final Shopify theme feature—alternate page templates.

For each type of Liquid template present in a Shopify theme (`product.liquid`, `collection.liquid`, `article.liquid`, etc.), you're able to create "alternate" versions of those templates, which you can use to selectively render different products (or different collections, or different articles) in a completely different way. This can be useful if, for example, some of your products have a demonstration video that completely changes the desired layout of the page, or if you want to create alternate layouts for text-based blog articles versus photo-heavy blog articles.

To create and use alternate page templates, simply create a new template file with the same name as the base template but with an additional suffix—for example, `product.video.liquid`. Once uploaded to your store, Shopify will display a template selection UI on the relevant page, from where you or the storeowner can select the desired template. See Figure 5-17.

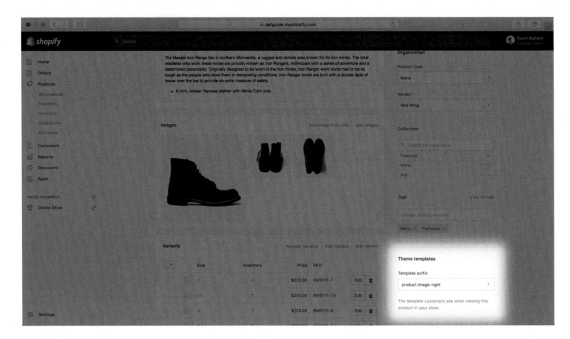

***Figure 5-17.***  *The Theme Templates section appears in the Shopify Admin when multiple template options are available for the displayed object type*

To demonstrate this in the example theme, I've created a `product.image-right.liquid` template (code visible in the example theme repository), which simply reverses the order of the columns on the product page to display the product information on the left and the imagery on the right. You can see how this displays on the store in Figure 5-18.

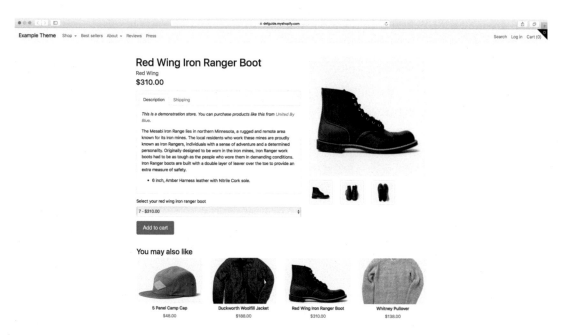

**Figure 5-18.** *A product page displayed with the alternate product.image-right. liquid template*

---

**Tip**    While the Theme Templates section only appears in the Shopify Admin for a select number of object types (products, collections, and blogs), *all* Shopify pages support alternate templates, and you can have as many alternate templates for a page as you like. To render these alternate templates at will, just include a `?view=` parameter in the URL—for example, you could force any product page on your example store to render with the image on the right side by linking to `https://defguide.myshopify.com/products/foraker-canvas-coat?view=image-right`.

One nifty use of alternate page templates is to render a custom representation of an object in JSON format (e.g., `product.json.liquid`), which you can fetch using Ajax from other pages where you might need to dynamically fetch product information.

---

# Summary

This chapter has been a deep dive into the design and implementation of product pages on Shopify stores. It started by discussing the importance of a product's information hierarchy and how the importance of different bits of product information changes depending on the store and the user's context.

With an example product hierarchy in hand, we stepped through the code required to put together a fully functional Shopify product page.

# CHAPTER 6

# Designing Home and Collection Pages

With the all-important product page out of the way, we can now turn to some of the other important components of a Shopify theme. In this chapter, we'll be looking at the design and implementation of a store's home and collection pages.

## The Home Page

As I suggested in the previous chapter, I feel that clients often focus too much on getting every little detail right on the home page at the expense of other steps in the customer journey. However, the importance of a carefully designed home page shouldn't be understated—it's just that an obsession with pixel perfection shouldn't lead you to ignore the primary goals of the page itself.

## Design Goals for Home Pages

When designing your home pages, you should try to achieve three primary goals:

- Convey to customers what the brand is
- Convey to customers what the store offers
- Convey to customers what to do next

## Conveying the Brand

"Brand personality," "corporate identity," "lifestyle brand." Whatever market-y term you'd like to use, it is important that a home page instantly conveys to visitors the nature of the store.

© Gavin Ballard 2017
G. Ballard, *The Definitive Guide to Shopify Themes*, DOI 10.1007/978-1-4842-2641-4_6

Users have strong expectations about how online stores in different verticals should look. While this doesn't mean that you should out-and-out copy the design of competitors and never innovate, it is worth paying attention to the conventions of the market—like common terminology, categorizations, and stylistic elements—to avoid innovating yourself out of conversions. Simply put, skateboard brands shouldn't look like Walmart.

The best way to get across your message is to combine a simple description of what the store does with some suitable imagery. (Yes, it sounds stupidly simple. Yet, you'd be surprised at how difficult many stores find this.) You can see the extremes of home pages that do and don't achieve this in Figure 6-1.

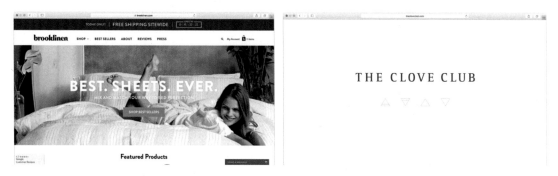

***Figure 6-1.*** *Brooklinen's home page (left) makes it clear what their product range is all about, while the Clove Club wins the enigmatic category at the expense of conversion*

## Conveying Your Product Range

Christian Holst of the Baymard Institute describes the litmus test for Ecommerce home pages as:

> *Does a quick glance over your home page adequately convey your store's product diversity? If not, first-time visitors may be drawing false conclusions about the scope of your site's product catalog.*

In short, if your store sells a wide range of products, but only a small fraction of them or a single product range is highlighted on your home page, customers may assume you don't sell what they're after and leave the site. The best way to convey your products will depend on the range on offer. If the store is more of a "product" company, selling a single line of products (e.g., Apple), then it may be sufficient to simply highlight a few of the store's most popular or new items. Conversely, if the store has more of a "retailer" approach and sells many different lines of products (e.g., Walmart), then it will be more likely to highlight and promote entire categories or product lines on the home page (see Figure 6-2).

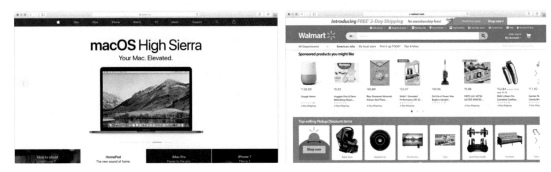

***Figure 6-2.*** *The home pages of Apple (a "product" company) and Walmart (a "retail" company)*

Note the difference in focus between the two stores—Apple focuses on highlighting a key product and links directly to it, while Walmart displays links to entire categories directly from the home page.

## Clear Next Actions

One of the biggest sins an Ecommerce store designer can commit is leaving a visitor to a site uncertain about what action to take to get them closer to a purchase.

Having conveyed a sense of who the brand is and what products are on offer, the next task is to make sure that potential customers have a clear path to being able to browse through the store's categories and/or drill down on specific products. As with the way you choose to display the product range, how your design achieves this will likely be dependent on the number of categories and products on offer.

"Product" companies can potentially feature their entire range at different points on the home page and link directly to the individual product pages in each case. Calls to action can be more specific ("Read more about the new MacBook Air").

"Retail" companies should instead feature key categories on the home page, encouraging users to click through and browse their entire range to increase the chances of finding what they're after. Stores with large ranges should design their home pages to place more emphasis on navigation elements and search functionality—recall the discussion of these elements in Chapter 4.

# Implementing a Home Page

As the design goals suggest, your home page often needs a high degree of flexibility to account for the different types of merchants using your themes, and to allow for the display of different types of content not directly linked to products or collections (for example, blog articles). Even when you're designing a theme for one specific merchant, their needs and campaigns will change over time, demanding a way to customize home page content.

Thankfully, Shopify provides a feature called *dynamic sections* for the home page of its sites, which allows you to design a variety of key components that merchants can then select from and configure to match their own use case. The following section walks through how we can create three different types of dynamic sections in our example theme—a "hero image," a "featured products" block, and a "featured collections" block (see Figure 6-3). A storeowner using this theme would then be able to add, configure, and rearrange these sections on their home page as desired to meet the design goals listed at the top of this chapter.

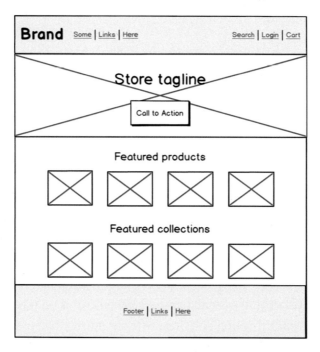

***Figure 6-3.*** *A mockup showing the three key home page sections we'll be implementing—a "hero image," a featured products block, and a featured collections block*

# Getting Started with Home Page Sections

Shopify uses the file `template/index.liquid` to render a store's home page. As with other templates, the HTML generated from `index.liquid` will be rendered inside `layout/theme.liquid`. Traditionally, the index template would be implemented the same as any other page template, with the HTML and Liquid desired for the home page added directly in `index.liquid`.

However, the introduction of dynamic sections on the home page of a theme means that most of the code used to render home page content will appear in independently-defined sections. Much like the `{{ content_for_layout }}` tag in `layout/theme.liquid` will be replaced with page content for the current theme, so too will a `{{ content_for_index }}` tag in `templates/index.liquid` be replaced with the dynamically-generated section content configured by the storeowner.

Because for now it's good enough having all the home page content managed in sections, we can update the contents of `templates/index.liquid` to simply contain Listing 6-1.

***Listing 6-1.*** Simple Contents of templates/index.liquid to Enable Dynamic Section Rendering on the Home Page

```
<main>
  {{ content_for_index }}
</main>
```

# Adding a Hero Image Section

If you recall, you first encountered sections back in Chapter 4 when designing and implementing the header and footer elements of your page layout. The dynamic sections we're going to be building for the home page are implemented in exactly the same way—the only difference being these new sections will be selected and inserted by a storeowner in the Shopify admin, rather than included explicitly through the use of a `{% section %}` Liquid tag elsewhere in the theme.

You can start by adding a section that allows the display of a "hero image," which is a common design element used to grab the attention of someone landing on your home page and convey some information about your brand. We'll also include a tagline at the top of the element and a button containing a call to action for the visitor. All of these elements (the image in use, the text content, and the destination URL) will be configurable by the storeowner.

We'll make a first pass at this by creating a new Liquid file in the theme, sections/ hero.liquid, and inserting the contents of Listing 6-2.

***Listing 6-2.*** The Contents of sections/hero.liquid

```
{% schema %}
{
  "name": "Hero image",
  "settings": [
    {
      "id": "image",
      "type": "image_picker",
      "label": "Hero image"
    },
    {
      "id": "title",
      "type": "text",
      "label": "Title"
    },
    {
      "id": "label",
      "type": "text",
      "label": "Button text"
    },
    {
      "id": "href",
      "type": "url",
      "label": "Button link"
    }
  ],
```

```
  "presets": [
    {
      "name": "Hero image",
      "category": "Images"
    }
  ]
}
{% endschema %}
<div style="background-image: url({{ section.settings.image | img_url:
'master', format: 'pjpg' }});">
  <h1>{{ section.settings.title | escape }}</h1>
  <a href="{{ section.settings.href }}">{{ section.settings.label |
  escape }}</a>
</div>
```

Hopefully, there's nothing too unfamiliar here. As with the header and footer sections, we have a {% schema %} tag containing JSON, which is used to define the configurable properties of the hero section. Those configurable settings are then used at the bottom of the file to output the HTML elements used to render a <div> element containing the image and text elements.

If we were to upload this section to the development store and refresh the home page, nothing would change. This is because for the hero image to be displayed, it needs to be added to the home page in the Customize Theme page of the Shopify admin. If you navigate to the theme customizer in the admin (refer to Chapter 4 if you've forgotten where that is), you'll see that you'll now have an Add Section option in the Page Content part of the left sidebar. Clicking that, you'll get the option to add a Hero Image section and can configure it with an image, text, and links (see Figure 6-4).

***Figure 6-4.*** *The theme customizer in the Shopify admin before configuring and adding a hero image section (left) and afterwards (right)*

Unlike the "static" header and footer sections implemented in Chapter 4, these dynamic home page sections can be used multiple times and can be configured independently or rearranged as needed. Like static sections, they also support the use of blocks, meaning we can give storeowners lots of control over the content displayed in each section.

We'll now add a couple more dynamic sections so that we can implement the home page layout sketched out in Figure 6-3. First off, we'll add a Featured Products section (see Listing 6-3), as `sections/featured-products.liquid`. When added to the home page, this section will ask storeowners to select a collection from their store, from which the first four products in the collection will be displayed. We'll also add a Featured Collections section (see Listing 6-4) as `sections/featured-collections.liquid`. This will display a list of collections in a similar fashion to the featured products section, but instead of displaying a predefined number of collections, we'll use blocks to allow storeowners to select exactly how many collections they want to display.

***Listing 6-3.*** Dynamic "Featured Products" Section on the Home Page

```
{% schema %}
{
  "name": "Featured products",
  "settings": [
    {
      "id": "title",
      "type": "text",
      "label": "Section title",
      "info": "Defaults to collection title."
    },
```

```
    {
      "id": "collection",
      "type": "collection",
      "label": "Collection"
    }
  ],
  "presets": [
    {
      "name": "Featured products",
      "category": "Features"
    }
  ]
}
{% endschema %}
{%- assign collection = collections[section.settings.collection] -%}
<div>
  <h2>{{ section.settings.title | default: collection.title |
  escape }}</h2>
  {%- for product in collection.products limit: 4 -%}
    {%- include 'product' with product -%}
  {%- endfor -%}
</div>
```

***Listing 6-4.*** Dynamic "Featured Collections" Section on the Home Page

```
{% schema %}
{
  "name": "Featured collections",
  "max_blocks": 4,
  "settings": [
    {
      "id": "title",
      "type": "text",
      "label": "Section title"
    }
  ],
```

```
    "blocks": [
      {
        "type": "collection",
        "name": "Collection",
        "settings": [
          {
            "id": "collection",
            "type": "collection",
            "label": "Collection"
          }
        ]
      }
    ],
    "presets": [
      {
        "name": "Featured collections",
        "category": "Features"
      }
    ]
}
{% endschema %}
<div>
  <h2>{{ section.settings.title | escape }}</h2>
  {%- for block in section.blocks -%}
    {%- if block.type == 'collection' -%}
      {%- include 'collection' with collections[block.settings.collection]
-%}
    {%- endif -%}
  {%- endfor -%}
</div>
```

With these new sections in place, we get some additional options under Add Section in the theme customizer and can configure two additional sections to implement the desired layout from Figure 6-3, as seen in Figure 6-5.

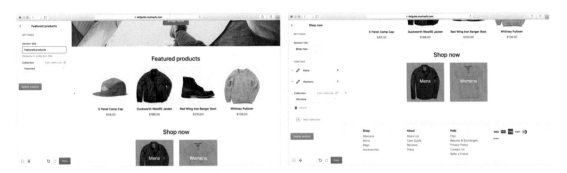

**Figure 6-5.** *Configuration of the featured products section (left) and the featured collections section (right) in the Shopify theme customizer*

With just these few simple sections, we've given storeowners a lot of control over the layout and content shown on their home pages, while ensuring each of these individual sections is consistent with the overall theme design. As you can see in Figure 6-6, storeowners can use multiple instances of the one section type to build up a home page that suits their brand and product range.

**Figure 6-6.** *A couple of different possible home page layouts built with the sections we've just implemented*

# Collection Pages

With the product page and home page put together, we can now move to the design and implementation of your theme's collection pages. These pages (also called "category pages") present a list of all products contained with a particular collection, so that a customer can view a large range of products at once before drilling down into what they're interested in.

All Shopify stores come with a default "All" collection (accessed at `/collections/all`), which contains all products listed on the Shopify store's Online Channel. In addition, Shopify provides a Collection Listing page at `/collections` that presents a list of all available collections. The collection listing page is rendered using `templates/list-collections.liquid`.

---

**Tip**   In some cases, you may not want the "All" collection to actually list all products available for purchase. For example, you may have a range of products with a "hidden" product type that should only be accessible to users with access to the product's URL. In these cases, you can override the default "All" collection by creating a new collection in the Shopify admin and ensuring it has its collection handle set to "all". You can then configure whatever rules you'd like to apply to the default collection, e.g., "Product Type is not Hidden".

---

## Design Goals for Collection Pages

Good collection pages should achieve three key design goals:

- Present users with a clear overview of the products contained in the current collection, or matched by any current filter.

- Provide users with sufficient product information to let them decide whether they're interested in a particular product.

- Provide users with accessible navigation and filtering tools so that they can refine the list of products to more closely match what they're interested in.

Collection pages are often treated as "stepping stones" between a customer's initial arrival on a site and their visit to the product page, where they add a product to the cart and continue through to purchase. However, their role in helping customers choose the products they're interested in through visual and information comparison shouldn't be understated.

As collections in Shopify can be associated with their own images and text content, collection pages can also perform an important role in a store's SEO by providing content targeting the types of keywords customers may be searching for (see Figure 6-7). For certain types of stores, collection pages can be even more important, as it's expected that customers get enough information to add items to their cart directly without visiting the product page itself (see Figure 6-8).

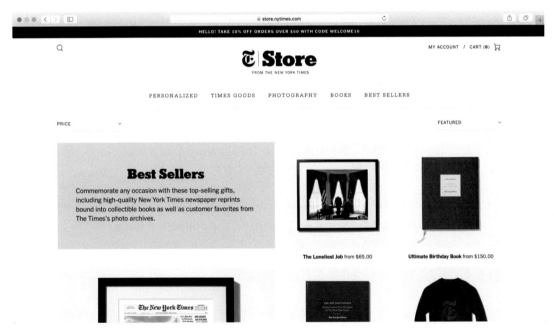

**Figure 6-7.** *The New York Times "Best Sellers" collection includes some collection-specific text content to provide customers with contextual information about the collection they are viewing and to help search engines direct searches like "New York Times Best Sellers" straight to this page*

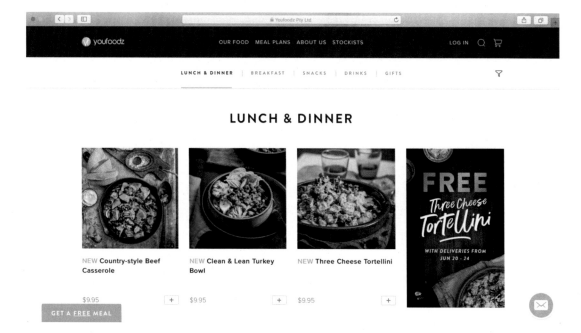

*Figure 6-8.    Youfoodz expects customers to add individual products (meals) to their cart directly from the Lunch & Dinner collection page. Note that they've provided an affordance for that in the shape of a "plus" button under each meal and that customers can still drill down into individual meals for further information if required to make a purchase decision*

I'll spend a bit more time discussing these design goals later in this chapter as we walk through the implementation of each feature on the collection page.

# Shopify Collection Page Concepts

Before we can jump in and start implementing a collection page to achieve these design goals, it's important to get an overview of some key theme collection concepts and understand how Shopify expects products to be categorized and navigated.

## Categorization in Shopify

It's common for Ecommerce systems outside of Shopify to have a "nested category" structure, with products being assigned to one or more categories that could exist at multiple levels of hierarchy. Shopify's hierarchy is much flatter—products can have membership in zero or more collections, with no inherent notion of sub-categorization. There are two types of collections—Manual collections (also known as Custom collections), where storeowners manually assign product membership, and Smart collections, where membership is determined by a set of rules (e.g., "Products with the type 'Shirts'").

Further product categorization can be achieved through product tags (discussed shortly under "Filtering"). I've seen plenty of attempts at squeezing a more complex categorization structure into Shopify themes using nested Navigation lists or collections linked through handle and tag names, but in general I think it's best to stick with the fundamental Shopify concepts. If a merchant has a product range that requires a more complex categorization approach, it's probably worthwhile investigating a purpose-built search and filtering application, plenty of which exist on the Shopify app store.

## Filtering

As hinted at, Shopify allows us to further refine products displayed in a collection via the use of *product tags.* A merchant can apply any number of tags to a product from the Shopify admin, and appending the tag name to the URL of a collections page will limit the displayed products to those that have the appropriate tag.

For example, navigating to `/collections/shirts/blue` on a Shopify store would display all products in the "Shirts" collection that are tagged with "Blue". Common uses for tags include colors, sizes, gender, product types, "on sale" or "limited stock" flags, and many more.

While you can filter on multiple tags (e.g., `/collections/shirts/blue+large`), it's important to note that filtering is applied in a *conjunctive* fashion (in the example, that means only products that are tagged with "Blue" *and* "Large" will be displayed). There's no way to apply a range filter (e.g., "Price between $100 and $200") or *disjunctive* logic (e.g., "Blue" *or* "Red") using tags.

## Sorting

Shopify provides several common attributes you can sort a displayed collection by ("A-Z", "Z-A", "Price: Low to High", "Price: High to Low", "Best selling", etc.). The desired sort order can be passed in the URL via a `sort_by` query parameter—e.g., `/collections/shirts?sort_by=price-ascending`.

Merchants can set the default sort order of products in a collection from the Shopify Admin, but there's currently no way to define a custom sort attribute without the use of a third-party application.

## Pagination

Shopify also supports a `page` query parameter in the collection URL (`/collections/ shirts?page=3`). To make use of pagination, you'll need to wrap the Liquid code looping over products in your collection with the `{% paginate %}` tag, as you'll see shortly.

Shopify currently has an upper limit of 50 products per page when paginating collections.

## Views

As with product templates, we can also create alternate product templates for our collection pages and swap between them with the use of a `view` query parameter (refer to "Creating Alternate Page Templates" in Chapter 5 for a refresher on how this works).

In the context of collection pages, alternate templates can be useful in allowing customers to swap between different views of a collection (e.g., a list versus a grid view). I'll cover when and why you may want to do this during the implementation phase, coming up shortly.

## Putting It All Together

Figure 6-9 combines all of these collection URL parameters into one and shows the role of each.

***Figure 6-9.*** *A breakdown of the options available when generating collection URLs*

The implementation of a collection page therefore becomes an exercise in (a) displaying a list of products in the most useful way possible to the user, and (b) providing a simple user interface for users to navigate through the product range via the generation and manipulation of the collection URL.

## Implementing a Collection Page

Just as the product template lives at `templates/product.liquid`, the template Shopify uses to render collection pages sits at `templates/collection.liquid`, which is the focus of the rest of the chapter. As with the product and home pages, the starting point will be a "prototypical" collection page layout, as shown in Figure 6-10.

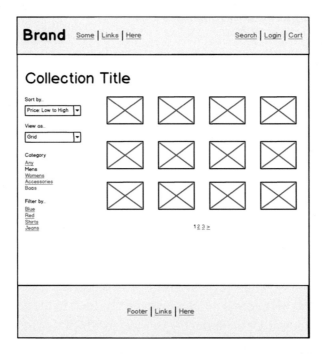

***Figure 6-10.*** *A mockup showing the collection page layout we'll aim for in this example theme*

As you can see, we'll be aiming to implement all of the key pieces of collection page functionality discussed earlier—sorting, support for alternate view styles, category-level filtering, tag-level filtering, and pagination. Let's get started!

# Adding a Product Loop with Pagination

To start off with, we'll add some initial code (see Listing 6-5) to `templates/collection.liquid` to perform the most crucial of functions—listing products.

***Listing 6-5.*** Basic Collection Page that Lists and Paginates Products

```liquid
<main>

    <h1>{{ collection.title | escape }}</h1>

    <!-- @TODO: Add controls for sorting, filtering et cetera here. -->
    <aside></aside>

    {%- paginate collection.products by 12 -%}
    <section>
      {%- for product in collection.products -%}
        {%- include 'product' -%}
      {%- endfor -%}

      {%- if paginate.pages > 1 -%}
        {{ paginate | default_pagination }}
      {%- endif -%}
    </section>
    {%- endpaginate -%}

</main>
```

The key points to note in Listing 6-5 is the product loop (`{%- for product in collection.products -%}`), which iterates over the products in the collection and uses the product snippet created earlier to render the product itself (`{% include 'product' %}`). The products available in this iteration loop are controlled by the `{% paginate %}` Liquid tag that wraps the loop. As you can see, I've chosen initially to paginate the collection in groups of 12. Twelve, eighteen, or twenty-four products per page is a common choice for listing pages, as they have a number of divisors that make it easier to create responsive layouts. In this example, with 12 products per page, we can display four across on larger desktop screens, three across on tablets and other smaller devices, and perhaps two across on mobile devices.

The other "new" thing we've introduced is the `{{ paginate | default_pagination }}` tag at the bottom of the page. As its name suggest, this handy Liquid helper takes the information present in the paginate variable (current page, total number of products, etc.) and renders it as a simple set of links that allows users to move through each page of the collection. You can see how these links look, along with the rest of the initial implementation, in Figure 6-11.

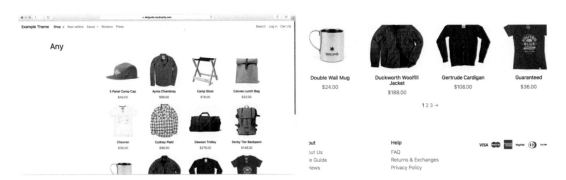

***Figure 6-11.*** *The initial implementation of the collection page (left), with a detail view of the pagination links rendered at the bottom of the initial page of 12 products (right)*

## Adding Sort Functionality

Next, we'll add support for sorting the collection using any of the predefined methods supported by Shopify. To do this, we're going to add a dropdown control in the left column of the collection template and populate it with a list of possible sorting mechanisms. In order to start with a JavaScript-free solution to begin with, we wrap all of our collection controls inside a `<form>` element and require the user to submit that form in order to apply their selected sort option.

Let's see what that looks like for the collection template in Listing 6-6.

***Listing 6-6.*** The Collection Template Once We've Added Sorting Controls

```
<main>
  <form id="collection-form" method="get" action="{{ collection.url }}">
    <h1>{{ collection.title | escape }}</h1>
```

113

```
<aside>
  {%- assign current_sort_by = collection.sort_by | default:
  collection.default_sort_by  -%}
  <label for="sort_by">Sort by...</label>
  <select id="sort_by" name="sort_by">
    <option value="manual" {% if current_sort_by == 'manual' %}
    selected="selected"{% endif %}>Featured</option>
    <option value="price-ascending" {% if current_sort_by ==
    'price-ascending' %}selected="selected"{% endif %}>Price: Low to
    High</option>
    <option value="price-descending" {% if current_sort_by ==
    'price-descending' %}selected="selected"{% endif %}>Price: High to
    Low</option>
    <option value="title-ascending" {% if current_sort_by ==
    'title-ascending' %}selected="selected"{% endif %}>A-Z</option>
    <option value="title-descending" {% if current_sort_by ==
    'title-descending' %}selected="selected"{% endif %}>Z-A</option>
    <option value="created-ascending" {% if current_sort_by ==
    'created-ascending' %}selected="selected"{% endif %}>Oldest to
    Newest</option>
    <option value="created-descending" {% if current_sort_by ==
    'created-descending' %}selected="selected"{% endif %}>Newest to
    Oldest</option>
    <option value="best-selling" {% if current_sort_by == 'best-
    selling' %}selected="selected"{% endif %}>Best Selling</option>
  </select>

  <button type="submit">Update</button>
</aside>

{%- paginate collection.products by 12 -%}
<section>
  {%- for product in collection.products -%}
    {%- include 'product' -%}
  {%- endfor -%}
```

```
  {%- if paginate.pages > 1 -%}
    {{ paginate | default_pagination | replace: '&laquo; Previous',
    '&larr;' | replace: 'Next &raquo;', '&rarr;' }}
  {%- endif -%}
 </section>
 {%- endpaginate -%}
</form>
</main>
```

The addition of this code results in a dropdown select being rendered on the collection page. Users are able to select a sort method and submit the form by clicking Update. They are then redirected to the same collection URL but with the appropriate sort_by query parameter set (thanks to the method="get" attribute on the form wrapping the new controls, which sends the user to a new URL based on the form input on submission, rather than "posting" it to the server). You can view the result in Figure 6-12.

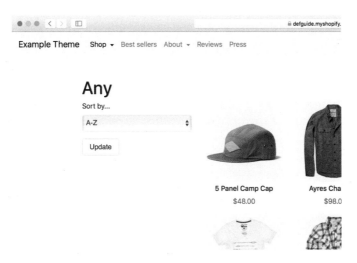

***Figure 6-12.*** *The addition of a sorting control in the left column of the collection page*

You may wonder why I've implemented this wrapping <form> pattern, rather than, say, adding a JavaScript event handler to the change event on the <select> element and updating the collection URL directly, which would arguably be less work for the user than having to make a sort selection *and* submit the form.

I am taking this approach for a couple of reasons. As discussed back in Chapter 3, building functionality that doesn't rely on JavaScript helps page load times, as well as keeping the site usable in situations where JavaScript breaks or hasn't yet had the chance to load. Furthermore, keeping a focus on the fundamental components tends to result in simpler, easier-to-manage design patterns. You'll see this toward the end of this chapter, when we use progressive enhancement to add a JavaScript layer over the top of the existing, simple, form-based controls. I think you'll be surprised at how little additional code we need to implement "dynamic" user interface patterns when we're starting from solid foundations.

## Alternative Views of Product Listings

As discussed, one of the primary goals of collection page design is to allow customers to effectively get a sense of the range of products in the current collection, as well as being able to compare specific products without having to drill down to the product page level.

The best way to allow customers to do this often depends on the type of product being sold and the context of the customer. A classic illustration of this is the decision on whether to display your products in a "grid" (how the example theme currently lists products) or as a "list" (with one item per row).

Conventional wisdom suggests that a grid view is most appropriate when:

- The appearance of the products is more important than information about the products.

- The products being presented are visually distinct from one another.

- Customers are less likely to be making direct comparisons between the products on display.

- Customers are more likely to be browsing than searching for a specific product.

The corollary to that is that list views are therefore more appropriate when:

- Information about the products is more important than the appearance of the products.

- The products being presented are visually similar or identical.

- Customers are likely to want to compare the products on display.

- Customers are likely to be searching for a specific product.

A good example of the first scenario would be a "What's New" collection for a clothing store. It's likely to contain completely different types of clothing (scarves, hats, and jackets) and customers will probably be browsing through without a specific goal in mind. In general, stores selling inventory where the visual appearance of the product is crucial are more likely to use a grid view (see Figure 6-13).

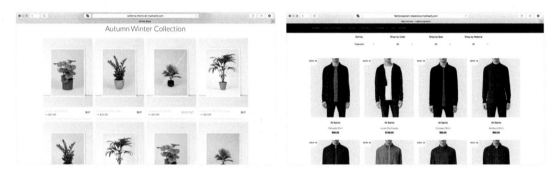

***Figure 6-13.*** *Fashion stores and others with a strong visual element to their products often use grid views*

The converse example would be the "LCD Television" listing in an electronics store. Televisions all look quite similar—the important things are the specifications (size, contrast, and features), and customers are likely to want to compare two or more options. Where the product details are more important, a list view is more likely to be used (see Figure 6-14).

***Figure 6-14.*** *Stores with lots of technical information or where comparison is important often use a list view*

It's reasonably common for Ecommerce sites to offer the ability to switch between the two types of views. Adding this sort of functionality is extra work, but can be useful if:

- You're uncertain about the types of product the theme you're designing will offer (common if you're building a theme for sale to multiple merchants).

- You have some product collections that are more suited to a grid view, and some that are more suited to a list view.

- You have large collections where a customer may want to narrow down their choices visually with a grid view before comparing a selection of products in a list view.

I'm always an advocate for keeping things simple and reducing the cognitive overhead of user interfaces, so if you think your collection page can do its job with only a grid view or only a list view, I'd stick with that. If you do feel the need to offer a choice between the views, make sure to add theme options (see Chapter 8) to allow storeowners to turn each view on or off, as well as set the default view type.

You should also take some time to consider how the information you're displaying to customers may change depending on the view type. If we consider the classic case where a grid view is used primarily for browsing, then "top-level" information like the product's appearance, title, and price is probably sufficient for a user to know if they'd like to investigate further. List views are often more information-dense so that customers can conduct more thorough comparisons from the collection page (see Figure 6-15).

***Figure 6-15.*** *The Kershaw knives site displays only the product image, title, and price in the grid view*

Changing to the list view exposes more detailed information like component materials and blade specifications. This makes comparison easier, although the size of the product images in the list view makes comparison of more than two products at a time difficult.

## Adding Alternative Views to the Example Theme

Working on the basis that we'd like to give the users of the example theme a choice of view, let's see how we'd go about adding a list view to our collection page to complement the existing grid view. To do this, we're going to use Shopify's alternate templates functionality, discussed in the previous chapter.

We start by moving all the existing code inside `templates/collection.liquid` to a snippet (`snippets/collection-view.liquid`). We need to do this because we want to share much of this code between the grid and list views—the sorting, filtering, pagination, and general layout of the page will be the same for both views and we'll want to avoid duplicating code whenever possible. Once that's done, we can include the snippet from a new version of `templates/collection.liquid` (see Listing 6-7). This template will be used whenever the collection URL includes a `?view=grid` parameter, or when no view parameter is specified. The default collection template (`templates/collection.liquid`) includes the collection snippet and specifies that we should use the grid view.

***Listing 6-7.*** The Grid View

```
{%- include 'collection-view' with 'grid' -%}
```

The alternate collection template below (`templates/collections.list.liquid`) will be rendered whenever the collection URL includes a `?view=list` parameter (see Listing 6-8).

***Listing 6-8.*** The ?view=list Parameter

```
{%- include 'collection-view' with 'list' -%}
```

If you haven't seen it before, the `with` keyword in the `{% include %}` Liquid tag allows us to pass an argument to the included snippet. Inside that snippet, a Liquid variable named `collection-view` will be available, containing the type of view we want to render.

Inside the collection-view.liquid snippet, the code remains the same as the original collection template, with two key changes. Underneath the collection sorting <select> element, we add a second <select> to handle the changing views (see Listing 6-9). This is inserted in snippets/collection-view.liquid between the existing sorting select dropdown and the "Update" form submit button. Then, the code around the output of the product loop (see Listing 6-10) checks the value of collection-view to render the appropriate product snippet—either the product.liquid snippet used previously for the grid view, or a new product-list.liquid snippet that renders a product in a single horizontal row (see Listing 6-11).

***Listing 6-9.*** Code for the New View Select Dropdown

```
<label for="view">View as...</label>
<select id="view" name="view">
  <option value="grid" {% if collection-view == 'grid' %}
selected="selected"{% endif %}>Grid</option>
  <option value="list" {% if collection-view == 'list' %}
selected="selected"{% endif %}>List</option>
</select>
```

***Listing 6-10.*** Updated Code for the Product Loop

```
...

{%- paginate collection.products by 12 -%}
<section>
  {%- if collection-view == 'grid' -%}
    {%- for product in collection.products -%}
      {%- include 'product' -%}
    {%- endfor -%}
  {%- else  -%}
    {%- for product in collection.products -%}
      {%- include 'product-list' -%}
    {%- endfor -%}
  {%- endif -%}

  ...
```

***Listing 6-11.*** The New snippets/product-list.liquid Snippet

```
<div>
  <a href="{{ product.url }}">
    <img src="{{ product.featured_image | product_img_url: '200x200',
    scale: 2, crop: 'center' }}" alt="{{ product.title | escape }}" />
  </a>

  <div>
    <h6>{{ product.title | escape }}</h6>
    <p>{{ product.vendor | escape }}</p>
  </div>


  <h6>{{ product.price | money }}</h6>
</div>
```

Figure 6-16 shows the result, with a new view selection dropdown in the left column and products rendered in the new list style on the right.

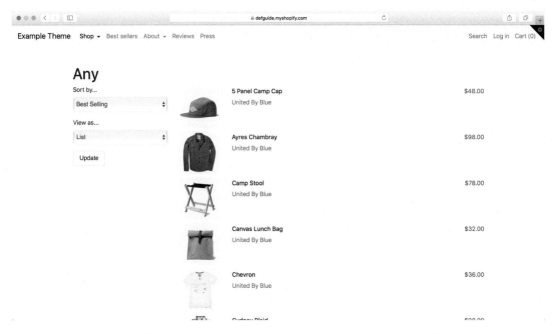

***Figure 6-16.*** *The collection page can now be displayed in a simple list view*

# Adding Category-Level Filtering

We've now implemented pagination, sorting, and view management on our collection pages. The last bit of functionality to add is filtering—a way for customers to be able to narrow down a range of products to just those they're interested in.

More than any of the other work we've done so far on the collection page, product filters are the most use-case specific. Depending on the product range in question, different filtering strategies and methods for grouping different filters together are called for. A store selling wine may have thousands of products and need to let customers filter on various combinations of vintage, country of origin, or grape type. A site selling a limited range of prepackaged meals, on the other hand, may only need to offer filtering on a single dimension (breakfast, lunch, or dinner) at any one time.

Most stores will need to have some notion of "category-level" filtering, a high-level way of starting to narrow down the product range to something a customer is interested in. As discussed earlier, this level of filtering is achieved in Shopify through *collections*. Adding category-level filtering on a collections page can be as simple as adding a list of links to each collection on your store, which is what I've implemented for the example theme in Listing 6-12. This code has been added to `snippets/collection-view.liquid`, underneath the sorting and view controls.

***Listing 6-12.*** Addition of a Straightforward Category (Collection)-Level Filter

```
...

<button type="submit">Update</button>

<hr />

<label>Category</label>
<ul>
  {%- for collection_option in collections -%}
    <li>
      {%- if collection.handle == collection_option.handle -%}
        {{ collection_option.title | escape }}
      {%- else -%}
        <a href="{{ collection_option.url }}?view={{ collection-view }}
        &sort_by={{ collection.sort_by }}">
```

```
      {{ collection_option.title | escape }}
    </a>
  {%- endif -%}
 </li>
{%- endfor -%}
</ul>
```

...

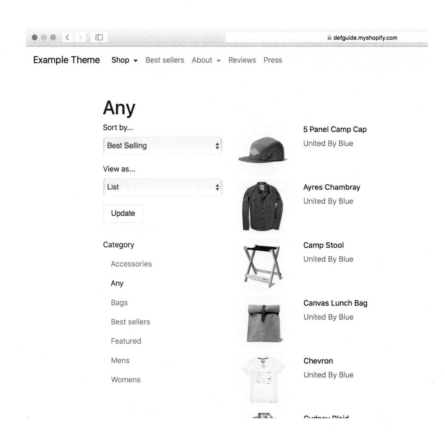

***Figure 6-17.*** *Category filters appear as a simple list of links in the left column. Only one category can be selected at any one time*

This simple approach lets customers easily navigate through each of the collections on the store by iterating through all collections and rendering a link to the collection page for each one. Note that when generating the URL to each collection, we include the current view and sort parameters to maintain a consistent experience when moving from collection to collection. Conversely, we *don't* include current pagination information, as it seems optimal from a user experience experience to move back to the first page as we completely change the visible category.

One potential issue with this straightforward approach is that storeowners don't have any control over the list of collections displayed, or the order in which they appear. We will remedy this at the end of the chapter, but for now let's move on to the next level of filtering functionality.

## Adding Tag-Based Filtering

For some stores with a limited number of products, category-level filtering will be sufficient. However, in many cases an additional level of refinement is required. This is where tag-based filtering comes in.

As you saw earlier when examining the URL structure of collection pages, adding a tag name to the end of a collection URL will filter visible products to just those in the collection with that tag. Shopify provides several Liquid helpers to make it easy to generate collection URLs for the addition and removal of those tags from the current collection view. You can see the use of these Liquid helpers (`current_tags`, `link_to_remove_tag`, and `link_to_add_tag`) in Listing 6-13, where I've added a list of tags to filter by underneath the category-level filter. Note also that I've updated the `action` attribute of the form to ensure tag filtering information is retained when changing the sort order or view. The use of the &#9745; and &#9744; HTML entities display a checked or un-checked checkbox, depending on whether the tag is currently active or not.

***Listing 6-13.*** Addition of Tag-Based Filters Underneath Category-Level Filters

```
<form id="collection-form" method="get" action="{{ collection.url }}{% if
current_tags %}/{{ current_tags | join: '+' }}{% endif %}">

...

<label>Filter by...</label>
<ul>
  {% for tag in collection.tags %}
    <li>
      {% if current_tags contains tag %}
        {{ '&#9745;' | append: tag | link_to_remove_tag: tag }}
      {% else %}
```

```
      {{ '&#9744;' | append: tag | link_to_add_tag: tag }}
    {% endif %}
  </li>
{% endfor %}
</ul>
```

As you can see in Figure 6-18, this code snippet renders a list of tags directly underneath the category-level filters.

***Figure 6-18.*** *How the collection page looks with the addition of a tag filter and zero (left), one (center), and two (right) tags selected for filtering*

Two important things to note with this approach:

- The tag filters here are being used in an additive manner. That is, as shown by Figure 6-18, we're able to filter down to just Mens products first, before adding a second Shirts filter. This is one option; it would also be possible to only allow a single level of tag filtering in a similar way to how we only permit a single level of category filtering.

- As you may have noticed from the screenshots, as we add filters, the list of available tag filters under the "Filter by..." heading reduces in size. This is because the tag loop `{% for tag in collection.tags %}` will only return a list of tags that are present on any of the currently visible products. This is usually the desired behavior as it avoids presenting tag filtering options that will have no effect on the resulting list of products, but if you want to maintain a consistent list of tag filters, you can use `{% for tag in collection.all_tags %}` instead.

# Progressively Enhancing the Collection Page

The collection page is now quite functional, and it allows customers to perform all the key tasks outlined at the start of the section. To wrap this section up, we're going to walk through a couple of things you could do to improve the user experience of the page.

The first of these is to add some functionality when JavaScript is available to users (*progressive enhancement)*. When we added the sort and view selection dropdown boxes, I noted that requiring users to click Update after changing one of the dropdowns was an unnecessary extra step. Thanks to the robust way we've built our collection page to date, with the addition of a few bits of JavaScript and CSS, we can add some logic that auto-submits the collection form when a select dropdown changes. You'll also see how to hide the Update button when JavaScript is available, as it'll no longer be needed.

Because the code required for these changes touches quite a few different files, I won't replicate it in full here in the book (as always, these code changes are available in the example theme repository online). Instead, here's the outline of the approach:

1. Add some `no-js` and `js-hide` CSS classes, applied to the `<body>` and Update button respectively, to hide the Update button when JavaScript is available.

2. Add a line of JavaScript to remove the `no-js` CSS class from the `<body>` on initialization.

3. Use JavaScript to capture the change event for the sorting and view selection dropdown elements.

4. In the handler for that event, auto-submit the collection form to apply the changes.

After implementing these changes, you should be able to load the collection page with and without JavaScript and see the same result as in Figure 6-19. Any changes to the sort order or view selection should be applied instantly.

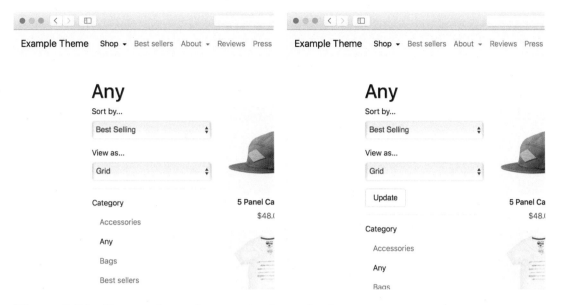

**Figure 6-19.** *Progressive enhancement in action!*

When JavaScript is available, parsed, and initialized, the Update button is hidden and changing a select instantly updates the view. Otherwise, the button remains visible and provides an accessible fallback.

A further enhancement we can apply is to avoid a full page refresh every time we make a change to our sorting, view, or filtering using an Ajax call instead. While I think the speed benefits of Ajax-driven dynamic interfaces are often overstated (especially if you've gone to the effort to properly optimize your theme), if added progressively on a solid foundation, you can avoid some overhead (the re-parsing of stylesheets and JavaScript involved with a page load) with relatively little work.

Again, I'll skip the full code for the sake of brevity and provide only an outline of this approach:

1. Use JavaScript to intercept the `submit` event on the collection form, which will trigger when the sort or view dropdowns change.

2. Prevent the default form submission, but make an Ajax request to what would have been the target URL to get the page content, then replace the current page content with the new.

3.  Use JavaScript to intercept the `click` event on the category and tag filter links.

4.  Using a similar approach as form submission, make an Ajax request to fetch the link's target URL and replace the current page with the new.

# Summary

In this chapter, you saw how to implement two of the key pages on any Shopify store—the home and collection pages. For the home page, you identified the key goals of the page (conveying brand identity and the product range) and saw how to build a highly configurable layout using dynamic sections.

You also learned about the design goals and implementation techniques for collection pages and the four key customer actions on those pages—view selection, sorting, filtering, and pagination.

# CHAPTER 7

# Carts, Checkouts, and Content

The previous three chapters covered the design and implementation of the components needed for a visitor to a Shopify store to discover a product (or products) they want to buy and add them to their cart. In this chapter, we'll be looking at how we can encourage customers to complete their journey from that point and make it through the checkout so that your merchant gets paid. As part of this, we'll be looking at how to minimize cart abandonment and strategies for maximizing average order value.

The final section of this chapter also discusses the "other" pages involved in a Shopify store theme—the content, blog, and article pages, which play a supporting role in driving product sales.

## The Cart Page

After a customer adds a product to their cart, Shopify's default behavior is to redirect them to /cart as a final step before moving into the checkout. Exceptions to this default behavior may occur if the theme you're working on uses Ajax-powered add to cart functionality from the product or collection pages, which typically keeps the customer on the current page.

In either case, the cart page gives a customer the chance to review their order and ensure they're happy with it before providing shipping and payment details. To ensure that as many customers as possible do in fact move on to the checkout process, there are a few design considerations we should bear in mind as we look at the cart page.

© Gavin Ballard 2017
G. Ballard, *The Definitive Guide to Shopify Themes*, DOI 10.1007/978-1-4842-2641-4_7

# Design Goals for Cart Pages

Studies show that on average, 69% of all online shopping carts are abandoned at some point during the checkout flow.[1] While no amount of design can rescue all lost sales, there are some key things we can do to encourage users to complete their orders. The breakdown of reasons for cart abandonment in the report cited previously indicate that the two biggest conversion killers for online stores are:

- The addition of unreasonable or unexpected extra costs (such as shipping, taxes, or fees)

- Checkout processes that are too complex or demand too much time and effort to complete

While the actual shipping costs and taxes charged by a merchant are out of the hands of the theme designer, we can certainly take steps on the cart page to ensure that customers aren't hit with unexpected or "surprise" fees during checkout. We can also make a concerted effort to simplify the cart page and ensure it's displaying only information that's useful to our customers and encourages them to take the next logical step (checking out).

The next section walks through the addition of a cart page that aims to meet these design goals in the example theme. At each step, we'll consider the specific design decisions in a little more detail.

# Implementing a Cart Page

Continuing the tradition of working to a "standard" design for the example theme, the cart page we'll be putting together will follow the layout pictured in Figure 7-1.

---

[1]https://baymard.com/lists/cart-abandonment-rate

**Figure 7-1.**  *A mockup showing the layout of the cart page we'll be implementing in this chapter*

You'll notice a few key design features of this cart layout:

- It allows customers to edit their cart, both by adjusting the quantity of line items or removing them entirely. This is important for both increasing average order value (if a customer would like or is incentivized to order larger quantities) and for reducing abandonment (if a customer perceives that adjusting quantities or removing an item from the cart is too difficult, they may leave the site altogether).

- It includes a note about shipping rates, designed to reduce the risk of hitting customers with surprise costs during checkout.

- It includes an in-cart upsell offer, which is designed to increase average order value through a spur-of-the-moment purchase decision. Care always needs to be taken with such offers to ensure that they don't detract from the primary goal of having the customer proceed to checkout, so the overall effect on conversions and revenue should be considered when implementing them.

## Adding an Editable List of Cart Contents

We'll start work on the cart page by adding a simple table displaying the current contents of the cart, as per Listing 7-1.

***Listing 7-1.*** An Initial Liquid Template for templates/cart.liquid

```
<main>

  <h1>Your cart</h1>

  {%- if cart.items.size > 0 -%}
    <form action="/cart" method="post">
      <table>
        <thead>
          <tr>
            <th colspan="2">Item</th>
            <th>Quantity</th>
            <th>Price</th>
          </tr>
        </thead>
        <tbody>
          {%- for item in cart.items -%}
          <tr>
            <td>
              <a href="{{ item.url }}">
                <img src="{{ item | img_url: '120x120', scale: 2, crop:
                'center' }}" width="120" alt="{{ item.title | escape }}" />
              </a>
            </td>
            <td>
              <h6>{{ item.title | escape }}</h6>
              <p>{{ item.sku | escape }}</p>
              <a href="/cart/change?line={{ forloop.index }}
              &quantity=0">Remove</a>
            </td>
```

```
        <td>
          <input type="number" name="updates[]" value=
          "{{ item.quantity }}" />
        </td>
        <td>
          {{ item.line_price | money }}
        </td>
      </tr>
      {%- endfor -%}
    </tbody>
    <tfoot>
      <tr>
        <td colspan="3"></td>
        <td><strong>{{ cart.total_price | money }}</strong></td>
      </tr>
      <tr>
        <td colspan="4">
          <input type="submit" name="update" value="Update" />
          <input type="submit" name="checkout" value="Proceed to
          checkout" />
        </td>
      </tr>
    </tfoot>
  </table>
</form>
{%- else -%}
<p>
  Your cart is empty.
</p>
{%- endif -%}
```

```
</main>
```

The contents of the table are wrapped in a `<form>`, and at the bottom of the page, we include an Update button. This allows customers to update the quantity of products in their cart by changing the quantity inputs and submitting the form. We'll also include a Remove link for each line item and a Proceed to Checkout button that serves as the primary call to action on the page.

Once it's implemented, a cart with a couple of line items in it should look like Figure 7-2.

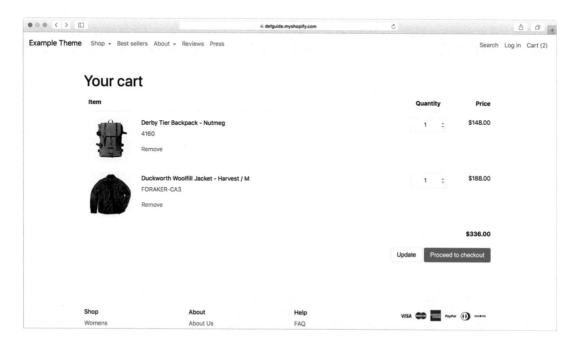

**Figure 7-2.**   *The initial implementation of the cart page as it appears in the browser*

As we did with the view controls on your collection pages in Chapter 6, we can use progressive enhancement to drive the update of line item quantities when JavaScript is available and avoid the clunkiness of having to click Update on the cart page. The full code required to implement this is available in the example theme GitHub repository, but the general approach is:

- Intercept the change event on the quantity inputs in the cart table.

- When a change occurs, use Shopify's Ajax API[2] to make an Ajax request to update the quantity of the given line item.

- Use the CSS classes we implemented for the collection page to hide the Update button when JavaScript is available.

[2]https://help.shopify.com/themes/development/getting-started/using-ajax-api.

# Adding a Shipping Cost Calculator

With the basic functionality of the cart page together, we can move to adding a note above the Proceed to Checkout button that aims to reduce the risk of surprises for the customers when they move through to the checkout. Because loading shipping costs requires some dynamic JavaScript, we can start by implementing a default, plan-HTML fallback option—displaying a static note as in Listing 7-2 and Figure 7-3. In Listing 7-2, the table footer from Listing 7-1 has been updated with a static shipping costs message. The element containing the message is given an `id` attribute so we can refer to it and dynamically update it later.

*Listing 7-2.* Table Footer from Listing 7-1 Updated with a Static Shipping Costs Message

```
...
<tfoot>
  <tr>
    <td colspan="3"></td>
    <td><strong>{{ cart.total_price | money }}</strong></td>
  </tr>
  <tr>
    <td id="cart-shipping" colspan="4">
      <em>Shipping and taxes calculated during checkout</em>
    </td>
  </tr>
  <tr>
    <td colspan="4">
      <input type="submit" name="update" value="Update" />
      <input type="submit" name="checkout" value="Proceed to checkout" />
    </td>
  </tr>
</tfoot>
...
```

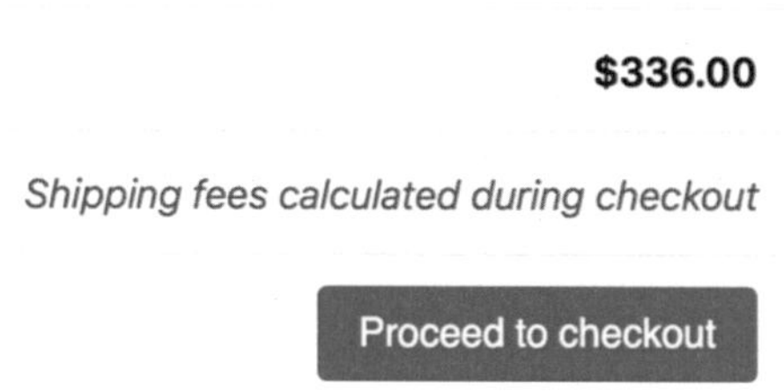

**$336.00**

*Shipping fees calculated during checkout*

Proceed to checkout

***Figure 7-3.*** *The fallback shipping message as it appears in the cart table*

With this fallback in place, we'll now implement some JavaScript that uses Shopify's Ajax API to fetch an estimate of shipping rates and display that to the customer. To properly estimate shipping rates, we need to have some idea of where you're shipping to (a country, state, and postcode)—information that we don't usually have at the cart step.

For the purposes of the example theme, we're going to keep things simple and only fetch and display a more accurate shipping estimate for logged-in customers with a known delivery address. In other situations, we won't perform any dynamic updates and the fallback message will be displayed. In a real-world situation, you could look to extend the code you're about to implement to fetch an unfamiliar customer's location via the JavaScript Geolocation API, an approximation based on their IP address, or simply a form requesting their address details.

The implementation of this functionality requires changes to three theme files:

1. First, we need to add a new `fetchShippingRateEstimate` JavaScript method in `assets/theme.js.liquid`. It expects to be passed the logged-in customer's address and the selector of a target element where the shipping estimate message will be rendered. It then does the work of making an Ajax call to Shopify's shipping rate's API and renders the result. This method is shown in Listing 7-3.

2. Because the details of any logged-in customer are only available to the core Liquid templates, and not the asset files, we need to pass the customer details to the newly-written `fetchShippingRateEstimate` method from `templates/cart.liquid`. This is shown in Listing 7-4, using a technique I call the "Captured JS" pattern, explained in the Tip that follows.

3. Finally, for the "Captured JS" pattern to work, we need to add a single line of code to the bottom of `layout/theme.liquid`, underneath all the other JavaScript. This is shown in Listing 7-5.

**Tip**   Good practice dictates that JavaScript is loaded and initialized at the bottom of all pages in `theme.liquid`, as top-loading JavaScript is one of the biggest sources of page slowdown and poor load times. However, there's often JavaScript that you may wish to load or execute only on specific pages—the initialization call to `fetchShippingRateEstimates` here being a good example.

In these cases, I use the **Captured JS** technique—using a Liquid `{% capture %}` tag within my Liquid template to store any page-specific JavaScript to a variable called `captured_js`. This can be used multiple times on a page as long as you're sure to output the previous contents of `captured_js` along with the newly-captured contents (see Listing 7-4). Your `theme.liquid` template can then output the captured contents at the very bottom of the page, ensuring any JavaScript libraries have been loaded before execution.

Note that Listing 7-3 exposes the method globally on the window object—in a production theme you might want to namespace this (e.g., `window.ExampleTheme. fetchShippingRateEstimate`).

***Listing 7-3.***   The fetchShippingRateEstimate Added to theme.js.liquid.

```
...
window.fetchShippingRateEstimate = function(target, shipping_address) {
  if(!shipping_address) return;
  $.ajax({
    url: '/cart/shipping_rates.json',
    data: $.serialize({ shipping_address: shipping_address }),
    success: function(shipping_rates) {
      if(shipping_rates.length === 0) return;
      var shipping_rate = shipping_rates[0];
      $(target).html(
        '<em>' +
          shipping_rate.name + ' ($' + shipping_rate.price + ') to ' +
          shipping_address.city + ', ' + shipping_address.province +
        '</em>'
      );
```

```
    }
  });
};
...
```

Note that Listing 7-4 uses the handy Liquid | json filter, which will take a Liquid variable such as a customer's default address and convert it into a JSON object for use in the JavaScript.

***Listing 7-4.*** The "Captured JS" Pattern in Operation at the Bottom of cart.liquid

```
...
</main>

{%- capture captured_js -%}
  {{- captured_js -}}
  <script type="text/javascript">
    fetchShippingRateEstimate('#cart-shipping', {{ customer.default_address
    | json }});
  </script>
{%- endcapture -%}
```

***Listing 7-5.*** The Bottom of the theme.liquid Has a New Addition—the Output of the captured_js Liquid Variable

```
    ...
    {{- 'theme.js' | asset_url | script_tag -}}
    {{- captured_js -}}
  </body>
</html>
```

Figure 7-4 shows the result on the cart page once shipping rates have been fetched.

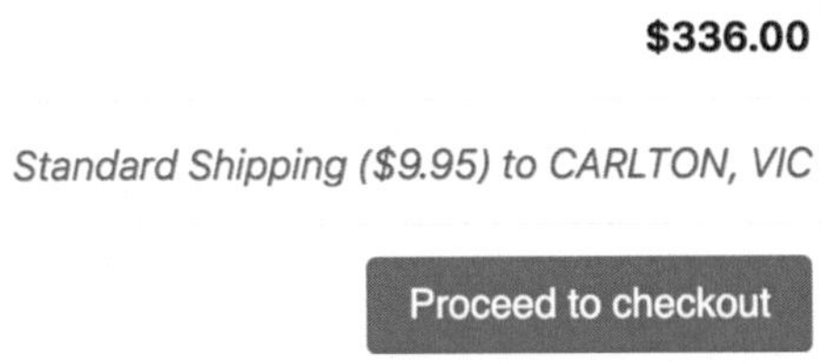

**$336.00**

*Standard Shipping ($9.95) to CARLTON, VIC*

Proceed to checkout

***Figure 7-4.*** *If a customer with a known address is logged in, the cart page now fetches a shipping estimate for their location and provides a more specific shipping costs message*

## Adding an Upsell Offer

The final addition to the cart page will be a simple upsell offer, based on the current contents of the cart. To drive this functionality, we'll use the following approach:

1. We will introduce a new "upsell" metafield that can be applied to our products (refer to the section "Managing Additional Information with Metafields" in Chapter 5 for a refresher on how this works).

2. On the cart page, we will iterate through each item in the cart to see if it has an upsell metafield set, and if it points to a product that's not already in the cart. If so, we'll display an image of the upsell product along with a button to allow customers to add it to the cart.

For this approach to work, we need to add a `cart-upsell.liquid` snippet (see Listing 7-6) and include it at the bottom of the existing `cart.liquid` template. It contains Liquid logic to iterate through the current cart and look for a product that's designated as an upsell but isn't already in the cart. As soon as a valid upsell is found, we break out of the loop, so a maximum of one offer will be displayed at a time.

***Listing 7-6.*** The cart-upsell.liquid File

```
{%- assign upsell_product = nil -%}

{%- for item in cart.items -%}
  {%- assign upsell_product_handle = item.product.metafields.theme.upsell_
  product_handle -%}
```

```
  {%- if upsell_product_handle == blank -%}
    {%- next -%}
  {%- endif -%}

  {%- assign already_in_cart = false -%}
  {%- for upsell_item in cart.items -%}
    {%- if upsell_product_handle == upsell_item.handle -%}
      {%- assign already_in_cart = true -%}
    {%- endif -%}
  {%- endfor -%}

  {%- unless already_in_cart -%}
    {%- assign upsell_product = all_products[upsell_product_handle] -%}
    {%- break -%}
  {%- endunless -%}
{%- endfor -%}

{%- if upsell_product -%}
<aside>
  <img src="{{ upsell_product.featured_image | product_img_url: '50x50',
  scale: 2, crop: 'center' }}" width="50" alt="{{ product.title |
  escape }}" />
  Special offer: <a href="/cart/add?id={{ upsell_product.variants.first.id
  }}">add a {{ upsell_product.title }}</a> to your cart for only
  {{ upsell_product.variants.first.price | money }}
</aside>
{%- endif -%}
```

With this final addition, the cart page is complete and should look like Figure 7-5.

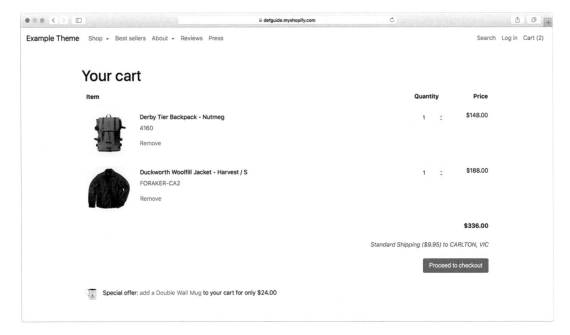

***Figure 7-5.*** *The cart page, complete with cart table, shipping estimates, and an upsell offer*

# The Checkout

Once a customer clicks the Proceed to Checkout button, they are taken away from the theme's cart page and to the Shopify checkout, where they'll be asked to enter shipping and payment information to complete their order. For security reasons, the layout and Liquid templates used in the checkout aren't exposed to theme developers in the same way as other page templates. Instead, merchants have access to several predefined settings in the Themes section of the Shopify Admin, allowing them to customize header images and colors to match the rest of their store (see Figure 7-6).

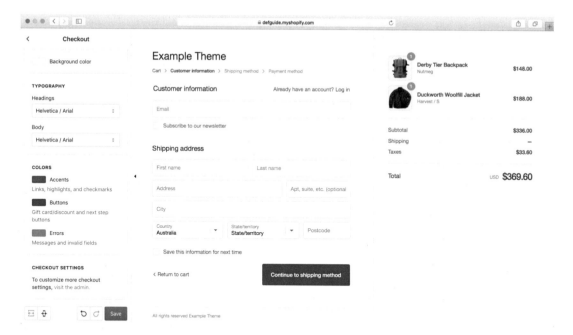

**Figure 7-6.** *Merchants can select from a limited range of options in the Shopify Admin to customize their checkout to match their theme*

The lack of customizability of Shopify's checkout is often cited as a major drawback of the platform. It certainly can be limiting—for example, it's not possible to change the ordering of form elements during checkout, capture additional information from customers, or use a custom font. The trade-off for this is having a secure, robust checkout experience that's being tweaked and optimized on an ongoing basis by Shopify—in my opinion, a net win for stores despite the limitations.

Within the scope of what's possible when it comes to the Shopify checkout, I think the most important thing to bear in mind is to reinforce **trust** in the store's brand and in the checkout process itself. The fonts, colors, and header images in the checkout should be selected to closely match the main store theme, so that customers don't feel they're "jumping" to another site.

**Sidenote**   Historically, customers would be taken from a Shopify store to a different domain name (`checkout.shopify.com`) during the checkout process, leading to a concern from merchants that this could affect conversions. Today, Shopify checkouts are hosted on the same domain as the rest of the store—but interestingly, during the testing for this change the Checkout team found no difference in conversion rates with or without the changed domain name.

# Customizing the Checkout with Shopify Plus

Stores using the Shopify Plus enterprise platform (as opposed to the "regular" Shopify product) have a much higher degree of flexibility when it comes to the checkout templates. Plus stores are able to add custom Liquid, CSS, and JavaScript to the checkout, although control of the layout and checkout steps remains with Shopify. These customizations need to be implemented on a store-by-store basis, as you're unable to ship a custom `checkout.liquid` in a theme for general use (in any case, checkout customizations tend to be quite store-specific).

While it's unlikely much of your early theme work will deal with Shopify Plus stores, at least in the first instance, it's good to have some checkout customization knowledge in your toolbelt. To help with this, we'll look at a simple but common checkout customization in our example theme by adding a store pickup selector.

## Adding a Store Pickup Selector in the Checkout

It's quite common to offer a "local pickup" shipping option to customers who live in the same country or state as a merchant's physical retail outlets. This is usually done by adding a Store Pickup option in Shopify's shipping settings, restricted to a specific geographical location (see Figure 7-7).

***Figure 7-7.***  *A store pickup shipping option as configured in the Shopify Admin (left); and the resulting shipping options presented to a customer during checkout (right)*

While this approach works for simple use cases, a merchant with multiple pickup locations can run into complications. Let's assume that your example store has multiple physical locations in several major Australian cities—Melbourne, Sydney, and Brisbane. While we could create a separate shipping option for each pickup location and restrict them by state, we would start to overwhelm the customer with options during the checkout process (see Figure 7-8).

***Figure 7-8.***  *With multiple physical locations available for pickup, the configuration gets harder to manage and the checkout process gets more complex for customers*

With access to the checkout.liquid template on a Shopify Plus store, we can tackle this problem with some custom JavaScript. The approach will be to:

1.  Set up a single shipping zone, called Store Pickup, in the Shopify Admin.

2.  Add some custom JavaScript to detect when a customer selects the Store Pickup shipping option, and when that occurs, render a custom dropdown element allowing the customer to select which specific store they'd like to pick up their order from.

3.  Pass the selected option as a cart attribute when the customer proceeds to the next step, which will store their selection against their final order.

You can view the code changes needed to implement this functionality in the example theme repository (while the code isn't that complex, it would take up a bit too much space to list it here). You can see the result in the checkout in Figure 7-9.

**Figure 7-9.**  *The checkout customization is now in place*

With the checkout customization in place, a customer now sees a single Store Pickup option during checkout (left). Selecting that option displays a second form input allowing a customer to select a specific pickup location (right), which then appears in the Additional Details section of the Order Detail page inside the Shopify Admin.

# Content Pages

You've now learned about the most crucial components of a customer's journey on a Shopify site—the home, collection, product, cart and checkout pages. There aren't the only pages present on a Shopify store—most stores will also contain "content" pages for things like the FAQs, about pages, contact forms, return policies, and the like. Many stores will also have blog content, whether for content marketing and SEO purposes or to document the release of new products.

While these pages are important for all stores, I'm not going to cover them in too much detail here. The principles and techniques we've applied to build the home, product, and collection pages can be used for page, blog, and article templates alike. Usually, most of the work with these pages involves assembling the content itself and building a design around it. Things like Liquid variables and filters, alternate page templates, and theme sections and settings are all accessible from within these templates, giving you a high degree of flexibility in the functionality and layouts you can implement.

You can check out the example theme repository for how I've implemented simple examples for page, blog, and article templates.

# Summary

This chapter covered the design and implementation of the final steps of a customer's journey to purchase something from the store. You've learned how to put together an editable cart page that includes some additional functionality like shipping estimates and upsells.

The chapter also covered the Shopify checkout and some of its limitations when it comes to customization. It touched briefly on how some of those limitations can be overcome for Shopify Plus merchants before wrapping up with a discussion of "other" content pages on your Shopify store.

# CHAPTER 8

# Theme Settings and Going Global

Whatever the situation, end users of your Shopify theme are almost always going to require some level of theme customization. To avoid forcing merchants to run to a developer every time something needs to change on their stores, Shopify themes provide for per-store configuration via a couple of different features—*theme settings* and *locales*.

For themes developed on behalf of clients, using these features to add a certain level of DIY customizability will save you plenty of valuable time in "five-minute fix" customer support. For themes you're selling to multiple clients, it's absolutely essential that end users be able to modify a wide range of theme aspects so that they can "own" their theme and customize it in a way that matches their brand.

## Theme Settings

As you saw back in the Chapter 1 in the section "Anatomy of a Shopify Theme," the configurable aspects of your themes are specified via a special JSON format, either in the `config/settings_schema.json` file (for global settings applied across the entire theme) or inside a `{% schema %}` Liquid tag inside a section file (for section-specific settings). A simple example of a global settings file is shown in Listing 8-1, with the corresponding UI displayed to the Shopify admin end user in Figure 8-1. Note that you can add Markdown-style reference markup to provide links to further information and avoid information overload inside the theme editor.

© Gavin Ballard 2017

G. Ballard, *The Definitive Guide to Shopify Themes*, DOI 10.1007/978-1-4842-2641-4_8

**Listing 8-1.** Settings in JSON Format for a Simple Checkbox Setting

```
{
  "type": "checkbox",
  "id": "favicon_enable",
  "label": "Use [custom icon](https://en.wikipedia.org/wiki/Favicon)"
}
```

**Figure 8-1.** *The result of the simple checkbox setting from Listing 8-1 in the Shopify Admin interface*

The settings JSON format and all the possible setting input types are well-covered by Shopify's online documentation,[1] so I won't recap them in full here. (Shopify also adds new input types on a semi-regular basis, so it's worth checking in with the most up-to-date source regularly.) This chapter focuses on a discussion of when it makes sense to use theme settings, an exploration of use cases, and some practical tips on how to use those settings in your themes.

---

**Caution**    Also residing in the /config directory of your theme alongside settings_schema.json is a file called settings_data.json. This file contains the currently chosen settings for a theme on a specific store instance. Try to avoid editing this file directly as part of your development process and make sure it's ignored in any revision control or automated upload processes you may be using. Failure to do so can often lead to developers accidentally overriding a storeowner's carefully configured settings.

---

# What Should Be Made a Setting?

Choosing whether to make something configurable by a storeowner via a theme setting will often be dependent on who the theme is being built for.

---

[1]https://help.shopify.com/themes/development/theme-editor/settings-schema.

## Settings for "One-Off" Themes

Themes being built for a specific client on a specific store ("one-off" themes) tend to have a pretty narrow focus when it comes to theme settings.

Given that you've presumably designed and built the site in close collaboration with the client, it's unlikely that key design elements like fonts, brand colors, and graphical elements will be changing frequently. The list of third-party services that the theme may need to integrate with (a mailing list provider, for example) is likely predefined, or at least under your control.

I therefore find that the sorts of settings added for one-off themes are time-sensitive feature flags or values—for example, a setting to toggle a site-wide banner with a custom message about an ongoing sale or holiday shipping delays, or which products should be featured on a key content page.

As part of the theme design process, I'll talk to the client to try to understand what parts of the site are likely to be time-sensitive in this manner and plan my setting accordingly. As a general principle, if you're unsure about whether something needs to be turned into a theme setting, avoid doing so until the client has asked for it to be changed a couple of times. (I find that given free reign, clients will want the ability to customize everything, even if there's no realistic prospect of it changing.)

## Settings for "Multi-Use" Themes

A variation of the "one-off" theme is a "multi-use" theme, where you're designing and building a theme for a specific client, but where that theme will be used on multiple Shopify stores. The common use cases for this type of theme are clients running multiple Shopify stores to service different regions (e.g., US versus Australia) or different customer segments (e.g., retail versus wholesale).

Unless the differences between regions or customer segments are so vast that a completely different design is required, it's very useful to have a single codebase driving all variations of a particular theme, with the settings on each individual store determining the final look and functionality for that region or target customer.

As an example of this approach in the wild, you can compare the retail and wholesale versions of the Colonna Coffee Shopify stores in Figure 8-2.

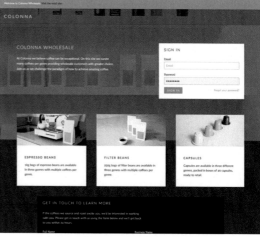

*Figure 8-2.*  *The home page of the Colonna Coffee retail page (left) and the Colonna Coffee wholesale page (right). Both sites are driven by the exact same theme code*

Both stores use the same theme, and the `settings_schema.json` file contains an option for `store_type` (set to either `retail` or `wholesale`) that the template files themselves can read and use to display different content depending on the result.

Other examples of theme settings commonly used for "multi-use" themes include:

- Whether to activate theme features based on the legal requirements of the region serviced (e.g., age verification or cookie warnings)

- Order minimums for wholesale sites

- Primary brand colors to distinguish retail from wholesale

Again, the best way to work out what needs to go into the theme settings is by having a discussion with the client and understanding their needs.

## Settings for "Distributed" Themes

At the other end of the spectrum to the narrow focus of a "one-off" theme for a specific client is a "distributed" theme—one that could be used by a multitude of businesses you have no direct connection to. This comes with the most number of headaches when it comes to theme settings.

Users are going to want much more flexibility and control, including being able to configure colors, fonts, and layout settings. There also needs to be more flexibility in the integrations your settings support—for example, your newsletter widget may now require settings that support the use of MailChimp, Campaign Monitor, and InfusionSoft instead of just a single provider.

The best advice I can offer is to start with some opinionated choices (*this* limited range of fonts, *these* mailing list providers, *these* layout options) and expand them only in case of repeated customer feedback, as each addition to your list of theme options results in a factorial increase in the number of things for you to test.

## Theme Setting Guidelines

The key to writing good settings for your themes is to think hard about the needs of your end users. Naturally, you're going to have to exercise your own judgment, but some general guidelines I suggest are:

- If your theme incorporates them, always make the following available as theme settings:

  - Any API keys used by JavaScript libraries (e.g., Instagram client keys)

  - All key images, including background images, site logos, and the favicon

  - On/off toggle switches for "additional" theme features like newsletter popups or countdown timers

- Avoid "god settings"—theme settings that affect a wide range of aspects of your site (the retail/wholesale theme setting used for the Colonna Coffee stores probably falls under this category—mea culpa!). Having a single setting that drives major changes across the site makes it harder to reason about the state of your theme or isolate feature change. If possible, break these down into more focused settings that control individual behaviors.

- Avoid specifying lists directly in theme settings, and instead leverage Shopify's built-in concepts like navigation menus, collections, and blogs. Having a single setting that points to a flexibly-sized collection (e.g., "Featured products") is much simpler than having many settings, each pointing to a specific product.

- Almost without exception, any configurable text content displayed to customers should be configurable via a store's language files (we'll discuss these in a little bit) rather than via a theme setting. This gives storeowners a single point of control for all theme text content and avoids missed translations or text changes.

# Using Settings in Your Themes

Within your theme's Liquid code, settings can be used just like any other variable, as per Listing 8-2.

***Listing 8-2.*** A Simple Settings Usage Example in Liquid Code

```
<header>
  {% if settings.display_site_banner %}
    {% include 'site-banner' %}
  {% endif %}
</header>
```

# The Iteration Pattern

It's common to have a group of settings you'd like repeated a few times. For example, if your theme has an image carousel on the home page, you might want users to be able to configure the image, caption, and link for each slide. The naïve approach (shown in Listing 8-3) is to repeat your HTML logic once for each repeated element. A better approach (shown in Listing 8-4) is to dynamically iterate over setting values.

***Listing 8-3.*** The Naïve Approach to Repeated Theme Settings

```
<ul class="slides">
  {% if settings.show_slide_1 %}
    <li>
      <img src="{{ 'image_slide_1.png' | asset_url }}" />
      {{ settings.caption_slide_1 | escape }}
    </li>
  {% endif %}
  {% if settings.show_slide_2 %}
```

```
    <li>
      <img src="{{ 'image_slide_2.png' | asset_url }}" />
      {{ settings.caption_slide_2 | escape }}
    </li>
  {% endif %}
  {% if settings.show_slide_3 %}
    <li>
      <img src="{{ 'image_slide_3.png' | asset_url }}" />
      {{ settings.caption_slide_3 | escape }}
    </li>
  {% endif %}
</ul>
```

*Listing 8-4.* The Iteration Approach to Repeated Theme Settings

```
<ul class="slides">
  {% for i in (1..3) %}
    {% capture setting_slide_show %}show_slide_{{i}}{% endcapture %}
    {% capture setting_slide_image %}image_slide_{{i}}.png{% endcapture %}
    {% capture setting_slide_title %}caption_slide_{{i}}{% endcapture %}
    {% if settings[setting_slide_show] %}
      <li>
        <img src="{{ setting_slide_image | asset_url }}" />
        {{ settings[setting_slide_title] | escape }}
      </li>
    {% endif %}
  {% endfor %}
</ul>
```

Not only is this code shorter to write, it's easy to scale when you want to add more than three slides. It also means that you need to update the HTML rendered for each slide in only one place.

# Using Settings with Preprocessed Files

If you have JavaScript or stylesheet files in your `assets` directory, Shopify will run them through the Liquid parser before serving them if they have a `.liquid` extension at the end of their filename, as shown in Listing 8-5.

***Listing 8-5.*** Theme Settings Inside an asset Field

```
/* assets/styles.css.liquid */
body {
  background-color: {{ settings.body_background_color }};
}
```

This is fine when you're working with simple resources directly in the `assets` directory, but often you'll want to do some preprocessing (such as LESS/SCSS compilation, or JavaScript concatenation and minification) before the final file is added to `assets`. In those situations, you need to worry about how your preprocessor will interact with the Liquid syntax you have in your asset files.

To work around these limitations, you'll need to either extract your settings-controllable style or JavaScript settings into your main Liquid templates, or write your SCSS and JavaScript in a way that passes the muster of any preprocessing tools and Liquid. Stewart Knapman of Lucid Design breaks down the problem for SCSS files in his post "Escaping Liquid in SCSS"[2] and provides some example workarounds such as Listing 8-6.

***Listing 8-6.*** Adding Settings-Driven Conditional Liquid Logic to a Stylesheet Asset

```
/* assets/styles.scss.liquid */
body {
  /* {% if settings.background-image %} */
    background: url(#{'{{ settings.background-image | asset_url }}'})
    center no-repeat;
  /* {% else %} */
    background: whitesmoke;
  /* {% endif %} */
}
```

---

[2]https://github.com/luciddesign/bootstrapify/wiki/Escaping-liquid-in-SASS.

The approach Stewart outlines here—wrapping Liquid in comments—is generally applicable to other forms of preprocessing such as Less and JavaScript.

---

**Note**  SVG files in the `assets` directory with a `.liquid` extension will also be processed by Liquid and can therefore use theme settings.

---

## The Default Filter

When your theme is installed for the first time, it's possible that several of your settings won't have initial values. To handle those cases, it's a good idea to use a default value in your Liquid templates to prevent generating invalid HTML or CSS. For example, if you make your body background color a theme setting, you might do something like Listing 8-7.

Note that you can also specify default values for settings inside your `settings_schema.json`—e.g., with `default: 'white'`. In general, I recommend setting a default in both places to avoid edge cases where no value is set.

***Listing 8-7.*** Example Usage of the Default Filter

```
/* assets/styles.css.liquid */
body {
  background-color: {{ settings.body_background_color | default: 'white' }};
}
```

# Going Global

To say that Ecommerce is a global affair is stating the obvious, but I have a word count to reach so I'll state it anyway. For theme developers, this means that our work needs to have out-of-the-box support for a variety of different regions, languages, and currencies.

# The Difference Between i18n and l16n

Do you know how long it took me to realize that "i18n" was an abbreviation (technically, a numeronym) for internationalization? Well, I won't tell you exactly, because it's embarrassing. Suffice to say it was a little while in to my professional software development career before I started digging in to how to make the software and web sites I was building accessible to folks without English as a first language.

So, as a quick refresher:

- **i18n** is shorthand for internationalization (there are 18 abbreviated letters, hence the 18) and refers to the process of making software (including web sites) capable of supporting multiple locales.

- **l16n** is shorthand for localization and refers to the actual implementation of a locale in to a software product that supports i18n.

For clarity, in the context of Shopify themes:

- **i18n** is the process of making your theme support multiple locales using the | t translation filter.

- **l16n** is the process of creating a specific language translation (e.g., Swedish) for your theme.

## Locales, Not Languages

You might have noticed that I've used the term "locale" instead of "language" in this section. This is because while language is probably the most important part of localization, it's not the whole story. While two locales may share a language, they may use different date/time formats, currencies, number formats, systems of measurement and temperature, and phone/address formats.

Most of the focus in this lesson is on language and currencies, but it's good to be aware of these other potential differences between the locales you're dealing with.

## Why Localization Matters

At the end of the day, there's no point talking about i18n if it doesn't deliver any real value to clients or customers. This section contains a list of some reasons storeowners may be looking to expand into new regions, demanding a new localized version of their theme.

# Acquisition

Have a localized site can open a store up to traffic from new places. Not only will Google find and add a site's content and product pages to a localized search index, but customers are much more likely to share content from a site if it's in a language their network understands and uses.

# Conversion

Making customers have to think when completing tasks is a sure-fire way to kill conversions—and figuring out how to get to the checkout in your second or third language counts as thinking. This is true even when there's a high degree of second-language fluency (for example, Scandinavians navigating English-language stores).

# Required by Higher Authority

In some situations, clients may just *need* to offer their store in multiple languages. This could be a legal obligation (e.g., government bodies needing to offer services and products in both English and French), or simply be a hard requirement from another branch of their organization.

# Empirical Demand

If you're still not convinced on this, I refer you to an eight-year-old thread on the Shopify forums, in which storeowners and theme designers have been arguing the case for i18n support in Shopify since time immemorial.[3]

People are keen for i18n support!

If you're looking to sell your theme, rather than develop one on behalf of a client, having a solid i18n approach can also be a great selling point. (If you're planning on selling your theme in Shopify's official theme store, it's mandatory.)

Showing that your theme can be adapted to multiple languages will give potential purchasers a lot of confidence that you've thought these things through, even if you don't have a translation for the specific language(s) they're planning on working in. Going the extra mile and getting the base of your theme translated into some common languages

---

[3]https://ecommerce.shopify.com/c/shopify-discussion/t/definitively-time-for-multi-language-support-19980.

in your target market (Spanish in the United States or French in Canada, for example) can also make your theme stand out from the rest.

# Go Hard or Go Home

When it comes to i18n, a half-assed attempt is much worse than no attempt. Plugging your theme content into Google Translate and copying and pasting the output is not going to lead to good results.

Think about any sites you've seen around the web with poor translations in to your native language—how much did you trust them? Would you buy something from them?

It's much better to have a theme with a single language done well than three languages that obviously had Google Translate as the author. Get a native speaker to provide your translations, whether it's someone you know and trust or by using a trustworthy translation service, or leave i18n until you have the resources to do it properly.

This is good advice to give to clients you're working with that are thinking about multi-lingual support as well.

# Limitations of Shopify Themes

Now that you're on board with this whole i18n thing and raring to get started building it in to your theme, let me deflate you a little.

There are, unfortunately, some significant limitations when dealing with internationalization on Shopify. In more recent times, Shopify has started to address these issues (the newer i18n theme features we'll be using shortly being a great example), but it's important to know there are still some hard restrictions.

These are:

- Storeowners can only set one locale at a time for any one store.

- Storeowners can only set one checkout currency at a time for any one Shopify store.

What this means is that even if you put in the work to support multiple locales in your theme, storeowners can only choose one locale to present to customers at any one time. There's no built-in way to give your customers a choice of language, or automatically present a translation based on a visitor's browser locale.

There is also no way to allow customers to pay in any currency other than the one selected by the storeowner in the store admin.

While these limitations can be irritating, in the remainder of this lesson, we're going to see what we can do within these constraints. I've consciously left any discussion of Shopify applications that provide translation features out of this discussion. It's good to be aware of them, but ultimately installed custom applications go beyond the remit of a theme designer in most cases.

# Making Themes Translatable

The process of ensuring your themes are translatable is very straightforward—it's just a matter of ensuring that all user-facing text content in your Liquid files is mapped to a "translation key" and then passed through the translation filter | t.

As a practical example, we can see how a link to the checkout would look in Liquid before internationalization (see Listing 8-8) and afterwards (see Listing 8-9).

***Listing 8-8.*** A Checkout Link Pre-Internationalization

```
...
<li>
  <a href="/checkout/">Checkout Now</a>
</li>
...
```

***Listing 8-9.*** The Checkout Link from Listing 8-8, Internationalized

```
...
<li>
  <a href="/cart/">
    {{ 'cart.links.checkout_now_text' | t }}
  </a>
</li>
...
```

The cart.links.checkout_now_text string is a translation key that identifies a particular section of the current locale file. Locale files are stored as JSON-formatted files in the locales directory in your theme, with one file present for each language your theme supports.

159

For a full account of the structure of translation keys, naming conventions for locale files, and some of the more advanced translation features like interpolation and pluralization, refer to the detailed Shopify translation docs at `https://help.shopify.com/themes/development/internationalizing`.

## Don't Forget JavaScript!

If your JavaScript files generate user-facing text like error or flash messages, you'll need to make sure they're translatable as well.

Translation keys inside your JavaScript files should end with _html (this tells Shopify not to escape their contents) and be passed through the `json` filter, as shown in Listing 8-10.

***Listing 8-10.*** Translation Filters in JavaScript

```
// assets/alerts.js.liquid
function outOfStockError() {
  alert({{ 'cart.messages.out_of_stock_message_html' | t | json }});
}
```

# Presenting Customers with Multiple Currencies

As mentioned in the beginning of this section, storeowners can only select a single currency for use at checkout. This can obviously be an issue for stores selling to an international audience, but theme developers can mitigate the problem somewhat by building multiple currency display support into their themes.

This solution won't affect the currency that's used at checkout, but it does allow customers to get their heads around exactly how much the products cost in their own currency. The gist of the most commonly used approach to this is:

1.   Ensure the HTML for any elements displaying price information in your Liquid files are marked up with a special data- attribute.

2.   Use a file named currencies.js (provided by Shopify) to obtain a list of current foreign exchange rates.

3.   Add a dropdown input with a list of supported currencies to allow the users to select their preferred currency.

4.  When the dropdown is changed, find all specially-marked-up elements and use the exchange rate information to convert to the given currency.

5.  Use a cookie to store the user's preferred currency for the future.

The specific code used to implement this pattern on your exercise store is shown in the code resources for this book. If you're using this technique, you should make sure that you explain to customers that they'll be charged in the store's currency at checkout even if they've selected a different currency.

# Summary

This chapter discussed the different use cases for Shopify themes (one-off, multi-use, and distributed) and the types of theme settings you might want to use for each. We covered the practical implementation of theme settings and discussed some best practices to make sure your settings are easy to use for merchants.

Finally, the chapter covered Shopify's built-in support for internationalization and translation. You learned how to implement translation in Liquid templates and learned about some of Shopify's limitations in this area.

# CHAPTER 9

# SEO and Social Sharing

Ever known a client that wanted *less* traffic to their web site?

Me neither.

Traffic is the lifeblood of any online store, and while it can vary greatly in *quality*, when it comes to *quantity*, bigger is usually better. The difficult part, of course, is getting that traffic in the first place.

Every day, Shopify storeowners experiment with hundreds of different marketing channels and tactics, trying to bring more paying customers to their sites. Covering even a fraction of these strategies is well beyond the scope of this book.

Instead, this chapter focuses on the specific things you can do as a Shopify theme developer to make sure that your themes offer the best possible starting point for merchants looking to market and grow their brands. This chapter covers a checklist of "on-page" best practices, discusses ways to provide search engines with structured information about a Shopify store, and finally looks at what we can do to promote the sharing of store content via social channels.

## Search Engine Optimization (SEO)

Driving quality traffic to a web site is a tricky, confusing, and time-consuming business—a fact that the huge, complex, and often slimy Search Engine Optimization (SEO) and online marketing industry depends on. The amount of misinformation and scammy business practices prevalent in the industry has often trained clients to treat "SEO" as a magical black box they pour money into on one end and get traffic out of from the other.

The good news is that as search engines have gotten smarter and less susceptible to sketchy practices and "gaming", sites are being better rewarded for the "right things," like providing better experiences for their visitors. In my opinion, this makes the job of

© Gavin Ballard 2017

G. Ballard, *The Definitive Guide to Shopify Themes*, DOI 10.1007/978-1-4842-2641-4_9

a theme developer straightforward when it comes to SEO—follow best practices when structuring your site, make sure search engines can read and understand your pages, and above all, make sure the site is accessible and usable for the human beings interacting with it.

# Off-Page versus On-Page

Broadly speaking, the myriad of SEO strategies, tricks, and techniques can be categorized into two main groups:

- *On-page methods* are implemented directly in a web site's code to aid in increasing traffic and click-through rates. Examples of on-page methods include ensuring pages have a sensible HTML structure, adding appropriate metadata, and making sure the site is fast.

- *Off-Page methods* cover everything else you might use to get someone looking at your site: e-mail marketing, pay-per-click ads, social sharing, or advertising on the side of the Goodyear blimp.

When we're wearing our Shopify theme developer hats, we are focused on the on-page category, as it's the only one we have direct control over. Off-page methods are just as important to merchant success, but could (and do) take an entire book to describe. If you're interested in learning more, I can highly recommend Moz.com, which provides a wealth of free and paid SEO resources. Their material is not only well written, detailed, and up to date, but honest and absent that slimy feeling you can get elsewhere in the SEO world.

The primary on-page methods covered in this chapter and elsewhere in this book are:

- Semantic HTML

- Keywords and content

- Structured data

- Performance (see Chapter  10)

- Layout and navigation design (see Chapter 4)

# Semantic HTML

The word "semantic" here just means, "use the various types of HTML tags for the purpose they were intended." This helps search engines (as well as accessibility tools like screen readers) make sense of the information on your pages and display the right information to users.

- Title tags (`<h1>`, `<h2>`, `<h3>`, etc.) should be used in order of importance, with the text content most relevant to the page appearing inside a `<h1>`, with subheadings appearing inside a `<h2>`, and so on. Titles should be under 70 characters long and unique to each page.

- Use HTML5 elements like `<nav>`, `<main>`, and `<article>` to help indicate the role of the elements on your page.

- Ensure each page renders a unique meta description (the content inside a `<meta name="description">` tag in your site's `<head>`).

- Make sure all images have defined an `alt="Image description"` attribute so that image-based search engines can index and display them for relevant search terms.

Shopify won't automatically validate your theme's HTML for you, so make sure you run the key pages in your theme through a HTML validation tool (like `https://validator.w3.org`) as part of your quality assurance process.

# Keywords and Content

In the early days of the web, search engines could be "gamed" quite easily. Relevance for certain phrases was determine by how often particular words appeared, meaning you'd end up with pages practicing "keyword stuffing," as shown in Figure 9-1.

> "We are the best dental office in Washington, DC. If you need dental work our dental office in Washington, DC would love to help.  Our dental office in Washington, DC is located at the corner of 1st and Main in Washington, DC.  We look forward to seeing you at the best dental office in Washington, DC."

*Figure 9-1.*  *Where are these guys located again?*

# Keyword Analysis

Fortunately, keyword stuffing tactics no longer work as search engines have gotten wise to them, but that doesn't mean that keyword analysis and research isn't important. Search engines aren't mind readers, so they do require indications on which words and phrases are most relevant to each page. Understanding the words and phrases customers are using when looking for a merchant's products is important in determining the priority your theme should give to different elements on a page. Ask questions like:

- Are customers likely to use brand or vendor names in their searches ("nike air pressure" versus "pumps")?

- Do customers search for products using a standardized part or model number (such as "MS2846728")?

- Are product variations like size or color incidental to the product, or a defining feature ("apple watch" versus "gold apple watch")?

# Duplicate Content

One thing that often trips up Ecommerce stores are "duplicate content" issues. Because many stores resell the products of others, merchants can be tempted to copy and paste the description of their products from the site of a supplier or competitor. This should be strongly discouraged, as search engines will pick up on this and treat your product pages as having much lower relevance in product searches.

Another issue unique to Shopify sites is that a single product can appear at multiple URLs (it appears at its "root URL" of `https://example.myshopify.com/products/ product-name` but also `https://example.myshopify.com/collections/widgets/ product-name`, `https://example.myhopify.com/collections/under-50-dollars/ product-name`, once for each collection it appears in).

Fortunately, all that's required to alleviate this is to make sure that your theme layout includes a *canonical URL reference* at the top of the page, like this:

```
<link rel="canonical" href="{{ canonical_url }}" />
```

# Structured Data

If you spend the time to make your site easy for humans to use and follow the standard conventions laid down in the HTML5 specification, automated systems like search engines and social networks will be able to do a pretty good job of understanding your pages as well.

However, there are things you can do to make it even easier for machines to understand the information on your site and provide hints on how that information could be presented to users most effectively.

One of the ways to do this is using one of many different types of *structured data,* which provide information in a standard, machine-readable format. This chapter focuses on the two types of structured data most relevant to Ecommerce stores:

- *Schema.org markup,* which allows Google and other search engines to read and present price, availability, review, and condition product information. It's also used for a few inventory feed applications such as Google Shopping.

- *Social Media markup,* which is used by social networks such as Facebook, Twitter, and Pinterest when determining how to present pages on your site that have been shared.

## The Schema.org Vocabulary

The *Schema.org vocabulary* is an open effort to provide a standardized way of describing "things" on the web. It includes a hierarchical definition of a wide range of objects and their attributes, from `TVSeasons` to `RentalCarReservations`. Most relevant to Shopify stores, it allows the specification of information about each `Product` available for sale on a site (along with information about the `Organization` that sells them and any `Articles` that may appear on a site blog).

Readable by all major search engines and many other automated systems, `Schema.org` markup is what drives the "rich" information that I'm sure you've seen in various search results, such as in Figure 9-2.

Walmart.com: **Lava Lite Classic** Lava Lamp, Purple/Blue: Decor
www.walmart.com/ip/Lava-Lite-Classic-Lava-Lamp.../16622926
$14.97 - In stock
Shop Low Prices on: **Lava Lite Classic** Lava Lamp, Purple/Blue : Decor.

Amazon.com: **Lava Lite 2124 Classic** 14.5-Inch 20-Ounce Silver ...
www.amazon.com › ... › Specialty Lighting › Novelty Lamps
★★★★★ Rating: 3.1 - 66 reviews - $19.99 - In stock
Ah, the lava lamp. One of the most beloved and recognizable icons from the 1960s and
1970s. **Lava Lite** resurrects the groovy gizmo, bringing it back to the ...

***Figure 9-2.*** *Product "rich snippets" in Google search results. Amazon's result not only includes price and stock information but aggregate review information as well*

# Microdata

Historically, Schema.org markup was provided through a system called *Microdata*. This involved the addition of special attributes and properties within a site's HTML elements that corresponded with the relevant data. To see how this process works, compare Listing 9-1 (without Microdata markup) to Listing 9-2 (with Microdata markup).

***Listing 9-1.*** Example Product Liquid Template Without Microdata Markup

```
<section id="product">
    <h1>{{ product.title | escape }}</h1>

    <div id="price">{{ product.price | money }}</div>

    <div id="description">{{ product.description }}</div>

    <ul id="images">
        {% for image in product.images %}
            <li><img src="{{ image | img_url: '100x100' }}" /></li>
        {% endfor %}
    </ul>
</section>
```

***Listing 9-2.*** Same Example Product Liquid Template with Microdata Markup

```
<section id="product" itemscope itemtype="http://schema.org/Product">
    <h1 itemprop="name">{{ product.title | escape }}</h1>

    <div id="price" itemprop="offers" itemscope itemtype="http://schema.
    org/Offer">
        <span itemprop="price">{{ product.price | money }}</span>

        <meta itemprop="priceCurrency" content="{{ shop.currency }}" />
        <meta itemprop="availability" content="http://schema.org/{% if
        product.available %}InStock{% else %}OutOfStock{% endif %}" />
    </div>

    <div id="description" itemprop="description">{{ product.description }}
    </div>

    <ul id="images">
        {% for image in product.images %}
            <li><img src="{{ image | img_url: '100x100' }}"
            itemprop="image" /></li>
        {% endfor %}
    </ul>
</section>
```

While widely supported, Microdata posed a few problems for web developers. Having to add these additional attributes throughout existing HTML markup added visual complexity to source code. Shopify developers could have the Microdata markup for a single product entity spread over several templates and Liquid snippets, making it hard to keep track of and maintain.

On top of that, the addition of Microdata imposed a tight coupling between the structure of a page's HTML and the relevant Schema.org data model, reducing flexibility and often forcing developers to add meaningless HTML elements to their page just to please the Schema.org nesting structure.

# Enter JSON-LD

The limitations of Microdata have now been addressed thanks to *JSON-LD* (JSON for Linking Data—http://json-ld.org).

JSON-LD decouples information about an entity from its HTML representation and allows it to be specified in a single location on a HTML page, making it the recommended way for Shopify themes to provide Schema.org structured data. It's added to a page as a simple JSON object inside a <script> tag, as shown in Listing 9-3.

***Listing 9-3.*** Simple JSON-LD Example

```
{
  "@context": "http://json-ld.org/contexts/person.jsonld",
  "@id": "http://dbpedia.org/resource/John_Lennon",
  "name": "John Lennon",
  "born": "1940-9-09",
  "spouse": "http://dbpedia.org/resource/Cynthia_Lennon"
}
```

For Shopify themes, my usual approach is to create a single json-ld.liquid snippet that contains conditional logic to display the appropriate structured data for the current page and include that inside the <head> of my theme's layout file.

For space reasons, I've skipped providing a Liquid JSON-LD example here, but the full snippet I use in most of my themes is available in this book's downloadable resources. Look for it at code/snippets/json-ld.liquid. It not only includes a good starting point for JSON-LD product markup, but also for the store entity itself and any blog articles.

---

**Tip**   While Shopify makes a lot of the product information you'd want to mark up with JSON-LD available in Liquid templates (such as title, price, and availability information), some attributes such as item condition or manufacturer URL don't have corresponding fields in the Shopify admin and, as such, aren't available in a standardized manner.

If you'd like to include this information on your Shopify store, a good approach is to use product and variant metafields to store that information and make it available to your JSON-LD Liquid snippet (see Chapter 5 for details on metafield use). The example JSON-LD snippet provided in the resources includes a demonstration of this.

One final thing to note about JSON-LD is that there are some types of `Schema.org` information that aren't yet supported. One example of this is the `Breadcrumb` entity, commonly present in the HTML of a site's navbar. If you want structured data bots to understand these navigational hints, you have to use the Microdata approach and add those attributes directly to the relevant HTML elements. This can be done in conjunction with JSON-LD on the page, so you only need to mark up the unsupported elements.

# Social Sharing

In addition to Microdata, there are a couple of other markup schemas that can be used to provide further information to particular sites, specifically social media platforms. The two main ones covered here are the *Open Graph Protocol* (developed and used by Facebook and now used by Pinterest for their Rich Pins feature) and *Twitter Card Markup*.

The benefits of adding support for these markup schemas is that these and other social networks can understand more about a store's products and pages, leading to a "richer" sharing experience.

# Open Graph Markup

Open Graph markup is simply a series of `<meta>` tags added inside the `<head>` section of your theme. The information you add through these tags is used by Facebook to generate the image and description of pages when they're getting shared.

These tags are also used by Pinterest's Rich Pins feature, which provides price and availability information so that users can purchase products from a Shopify store directly from Pinterest.

# Adding Open Graph Markup

For Shopify themes, we're primarily concerned with adding Open Graph information to our product pages and (if we have a blog) our article pages. These are the pages that we want to make sure Facebook and Pinterest can extract plenty of information from.

As with JSON-LD markup, I typically use a Liquid snippet to handle Open Graph markup, then include that snippet in the <head> portion of my layout file, something like Listings 9-4 and 9-5. In Listing 9-4, note the prefix attribute on the <html> element, which is required to indicate we're using the Open Graph schema. For the sake of brevity, I've cut out the Open Graph markup for the article templates in the logic block in Listing 9-5. The file in the resources section bundled with the course has the full code for that section.

***Listing 9-4.*** Example layout/theme.liquid

```
<html lang="en" prefix="og: http://ogp.me/ns#">
  <head>
    <!-- ... standard <meta> tags, stylesheet includes ... -->

    <!-- Include Open Graph Snippet -->
    {% include 'head-open-graph' %}
  </head>
```

***Listing 9-5.*** Example snippets/open-graph.liquid Code

```
<!-- This first tag first tag should be present on all pages. -->
<meta property="og:site_name" content="{{ shop.name | escape }}" />

<!-- Now we check to see if we're on a product page, and add product-
specific open graph tags if so. -->
{% if template contains 'product' %}
  <!-- Describe the basic properties of the product in the Open Graph
  schema. -->
  <meta property="og:type" content="product" />
  <meta property="og:title" content="{{ product.title | escape }}" />
  <meta property="og:description" content="{{ product.description |
  strip_html | truncatewords: 100, '' | escape }}" />
  <meta property="og:url" content="{{ canonical_url }}" />
```

```
<!-- Describe the product images. Use to avoid Facebook just using the
first image it finds on the page when sharing. -->
{% for image in product.images limit:6 %}
<meta property="og:image" content="http:{{ image | product_img_url:
'grande' }}" />
{% endfor %}

<!-- Provide price & availability information, which at the moment is
just used by Pinterest rich pins. -->
<meta property="og:price:amount" content="{{ product.price | money_
without_currency }}" />
<meta property="og:price:currency" content="{{ shop.currency }}" />
{% if product.compare_at_price_max %}
<meta property="og:price:standard_amount" content="{{ product.compare_at_
price_max | money_without_currency }}" />
{% endif %}
<meta property="og:availability" content="{% if product.available %}
instock{% else %}{% endif %}" />
{% elsif template contains 'article' %}
  <!-- Open graph markup for articles would go here. -->
{% endif %}
```

## Testing Open Graph Markup

Checking that your Open Graph markup is working properly is easy with Facebook's Open Graph debugging tool (https://developers.facebook.com/tools/debug). You just need to enter the URL of the page you'd like to test and click Debug to get a report on the information Facebook could extract.

---

**Note**    The Open Graph debugging tool *won't work* if the store you're developing on is password protected! This is because Facebook needs to be able to request the page in order to read your Open Graph markup.

---

It's also worth checking how things look when you start the sharing process on Facebook or Pinterest, as shown in Figure 9-3.

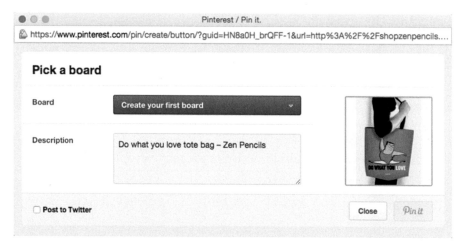

*Figure 9-3.* *The correct image and description has been extracted from Open Graph tags*

Doing this final test will let you see exactly what others will see when your products or articles are shared, including how images are retrieved and cropped, and any text information that's being truncated.

It's important to note that Facebook often caches Open Graph information, so if you're seeing incorrect or stale data, use the debugging tool to fetch the URL in question and then click the Fetch New Scrape Information button to force a refresh.

# Twitter Card Markup

Twitter Card markup provides a similar function to Open Graph markup, in that it allows Twitter to display "richer" information when pages from a store are being shared. The process to add the markup itself is pretty much identical to that used for Open Graph data, with just a couple of additional steps to test and validate the result.

---

**Note**   A Twitter account is required to add Twitter Card support to your Shopify themes.

---

# Adding Twitter Card Markup

First, we need to add the required markup, which like Open Graph markup, takes the form of a series of <meta> tags inside the <head>. Again, I tend to use a Liquid snippet to keep my Twitter card markup separate, as per Listings 9-6 and 9-7. Again, for the sake of brevity, the code-handling article templates in Listing 9-7 are omitted and viewable in full in the book's resources section.

***Listing 9-6.*** Example layout/theme.liquid, with the Twitter Card Markup Snippet Being Included

```
<html lang="en" prefix="og: http://ogp.me/ns#">
  <head>
    <!-- ... standard <meta> tags, stylesheet includes ... -->

    <!-- Include Open Graph Snippet -->
    {% include 'head-open-graph' %}

    <!-- Include Twitter Cards Snippet -->
    {% include 'head-twitter-cards' %}
  </head>
```

***Listing 9-7.*** Example snippets/twitter-card.liquid

```
{% if template contains 'product' %}
  <meta name="twitter:card" content="product" />
  <meta name="twitter:title" content="{{ product.title | escape }}" />
  <meta name="twitter:description" content="{{ product.description | strip_
  html | strip_newlines | truncatewords: 60, '' | escape }}" />
  <meta name="twitter:image" content="http:{{ product.featured_image.src |
  product_img_url: 'grande' }}" />
  <meta name="twitter:label1" content="Price" />
  <meta name="twitter:data1" content="{% if product.price_varies %}From {%
  endif %}{{ product.price | money_with_currency | strip_html }}" />
  {% if product.vendor == blank %}
  <meta name="twitter:label2" content="Availability" />
  <meta name="twitter:data2" content="In stock" />
  {% else %}
```

```
  <meta name="twitter:label2" content="Brand" />
  <meta name="twitter:data2" content="{{ product.vendor | escape }}" />
  {% endif %}
{% elsif template contains 'article' %}
  <!-- Twitter card markup for articles would go here. -->
{% endif %}
```

## Validating Twitter Card Markup

Unlike Open Graph markup, you need to "validate" your new markup before Twitter will use it.

To do that, simply head to Twitter's Card Validator at `https://cards-dev.twitter.com/validator` (you'll need to be logged in to Twitter). Select Product from the Card Catalog, then select the Validate & Apply tab and enter the URL of any of the product pages on your site.

Click Go and you should see confirmation that your card markup has been validated, along with a preview of what it will look like when someone shares a product from your theme, as shown in Figure 9-4.

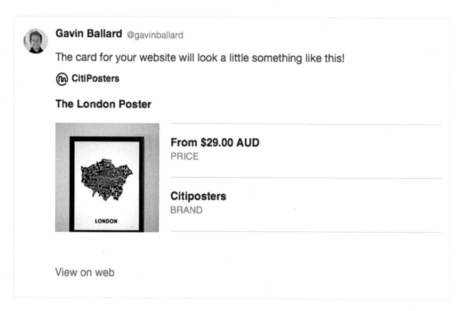

***Figure 9-4.*** *The Twitter Card validator will show you a preview based on extracted data*

# Caring about Sharing

Once you've gone to the effort of setting up this markup, you're going to want to take advantage of it by encouraging visitors to your site to share your products and content pages.

## Deciding Which Share Options to Support

First, you should recognize that "the more the merrier" isn't a great catchphrase when it comes to sharing widgets. Instead, sites tend to do better with social traffic when they focus on a few key social networks, rather than slapping a barrage of icons on their product pages (see Figure 9-5).

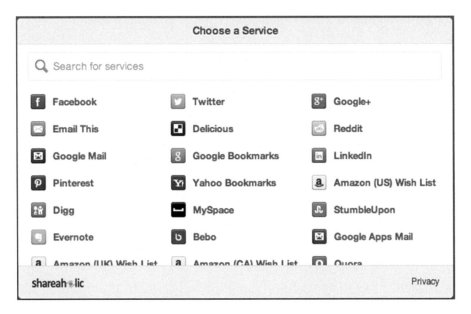

***Figure 9-5.*** *Scattergun approaches to sharing like this are rarely effective or engaged with by users*

Users are easily overwhelmed by choice, so making that choice simpler ("Do I share to Facebook or Twitter?") makes it more likely they'll take one of these actions instead of giving up entirely. Putting the focus on two or three networks also makes it easier for the storeowner to manage and engage people on those networks while running the store without being spread too thin.

If you're working with a specific client, a conversation with them should help you both work out which networks are going to be the most beneficial for them.[1] More niche or geographically-specific platforms might be important too, depending on the context.

If you're building a theme to be used by many different stores, then you should add support for all the major social networks and allow storeowners to toggle them on and off in the theme's settings page (refer to Chapter 8 on theme setting customization).

Regardless of which networks you choose to focus on, I strongly recommend giving users an easy way to share your pages via email. While not everyone may be accustomed to the social networks you're using, email is ubiquitous, and is the most common way of sharing a product with a specific person. Adding email sharing support can be as simple as adding a `mailto:` link with a blank recipient and a short pre-populated subject and body, letting the users send a message through their own mail clients.

## Integrating Sharing

All major social networks allow you to integrate sharing buttons very easily, often through a small JavaScript snippet. However, there are two major issues with using these default buttons:

- They're unlikely to match the design aesthetic of your theme

- They often come with a performance overhead and can slow down your site

The first can be an issue if the mismatch between the buttons and the rest of your page ends up drawing focus away from the primary piece of content on the page. The second is a usability issue, especially on mobile devices, where adding four or five scripts (which in turn often load additional scripts) kills performance.

Fortunately, the solution to both problems is quite simple! All social networks allow users to trigger a share action through a simple `<a href="">` link, which you can of course style however you like (see Figure 9-6 for example of how this has been done in Shopify's Pop theme).

---

[1]Kevan Lee's epic blog post called "How to Choose the Right Social Network for Your Business" provides some excellent guidance on this: `https://blog.bufferapp.com/how-to-choose-a-social-network`.

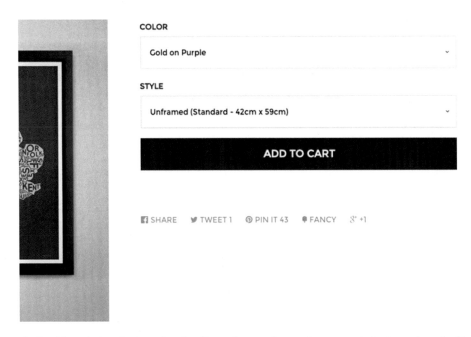

**Figure 9-6.** *Sharing triggers in the Pop theme have been restyled as simple links that match the aesthetic*

Building up the URL for the href attribute for use on the different social networks can be a little tricky. Here's an example of how I'd do it in Liquid for a Twitter share link:

```
<a href="http://twitter.com/share?text={{ page.title | url_param_escape
}}&url={{ canonical_url | url_param_escape }}" target="_blank">
  Tweet this!
</a>
```

Twitter's a pretty simple use case, as it only requires us to pass the text and URL parameters. Some networks, like LinkedIn, expect more parameters.

The code/snippets/social-share.liquid example in the resources bundled with the book includes a pattern for share links that handles multiple social networks, as well as adapting to the type of page (product, article, or content page) it's being used on, which you're welcome to repurpose for your own themes.

---

**EXERCISE: SEO AND SOCIAL SHARING**

Following each section in this chapter, walk through your exercise theme and ensure that it conforms to SEO best practices and that it's configured for social sharing.

Some of the things you should check are:

- Every page has an `<h1>` header and a `meta` description.

- Your `theme.liquid` defines a canonical URL for every page, using the Liquid `{{ canonical_url }}` tag.

- All images define appropriate `alt` attributes.

- `Schema.org` markup is provided on index, product, and articles pages, either through Microdata or JSON-LD.

- Product and article pages define Open Graph and Twitter Card markup.

- Products are easily shareable via on-page links.

Feel free to use the JSON-LD, Open Graph, Twitter Card, and Social Sharing snippets provided in the downloadable resources to achieve this. Just make sure you take a couple of minutes to walk through the code so that you're clear about what each snippet is doing.

---

# Summary

This chapter discussed the difference between on-page and off-page SEO. It then focused on techniques for improving on-page SEO in your themes, as they are the elements most commonly under our control as designers and developers.

The chapter also looked at ways to help customers share content from themes and looked at which sharing mechanisms it makes sense for your theme to support.

# CHAPTER 10

# Performance

This chapter explains theme performance—why it's important, how to measure it, and how to improve it. It discussed techniques that we can use to both reduce initial load times and improve the perceived responsiveness of a Shopify storefront.

While it pays dividends to be thinking about these ideas from day one of your theme design, the techniques discussed here are equally useful for existing themes that need some fat trimmed.

## Why Performance Matters

Way, way back in the olden days of the web (2009), Eric Schurman at Bing and Jake Brutlag at Google ran a series of experiments to see how their users responded to controlled increases in server response time.[1]

The results were compelling: in Google's case, an added delay of less than half a second led to a 0.6% drop in user engagement. Bing went even further and subjected their test users to a full two-second delay and saw engagement (and revenue per user) drop by over 4%. Their conclusion was that the phrase "speed matters" is not just lip service, and that "delays of under half a second impact business metrics."

This performance impact isn't something that's just confined to lab experiments, either:

- Mozilla shaved 2.2 seconds from their page load time and downloads increased by 15.4%.

- Barack Obama's campaign sped up their site by 60% and donations increased by 14%.

---

[1] Their report, delivered at the 2009 Velocity conference, can be found at `http://velocityconf.com/velocity2009/public/schedule/detail/8523`.

G. Ballard, *The Definitive Guide to Shopify Themes*, DOI 10.1007/978-1-4842-2641-4_10

In the context of Ecommerce today, I feel that site performance is more important than ever. As more and more businesses move to the web, consumers have more choices on where to spend their money online, and their patience for less-than-optimal purchasing experiences decreases.

*Consumers are expecting a faster web. Businesses succeed with a faster web.*

—Steve Souders, "How Fast Are We Going Now?"[2]

It can be tempting to dismiss this type of performance concern by pointing to devices that are becoming more and more powerful and Internet connections that are offering more and more bandwidth. I think this is dangerous thinking, for a couple of reasons:

- Since 2014, the majority of traffic to Shopify stores has been on mobile devices, where processing power isn't as prevalent and 3G (or slower) connections are spotty.

- There's a great deal of growth in Ecommerce in developing markets where the demand for online sales is high but Internet connections are often lagging.

- Even in developed countries, it's common to be shopping online with a poor network connection (I'm writing this sentence right now in a Swedish café with pretty lackluster WiFi).

- With the rise of the Internet of things, the number of Internet-capable but low-power devices (think TVs or fridges) that customers could be loading your sites on is increasing.

Moreover, ourselves yourself of responsibility for the performance of our Shopify themes in the first place makes it easy for our work to snowball into bloated monstrosities of sites.

---

[2]http://www.stevesouders.com/blog/2013/05/09/how-fast-are-we-going-now/.

# Why Performance Gets Ignored

If you're doing conversion rate optimization for a client and get a lift of 1%, that's a huge win. You'll be popping champagne and discussing what the business is going to be doing with the tens of thousands of dollars you just made them (hopefully cutting you a bonus check, but that's wishful thinking).

So, considering that a poorly performing web site can have a negative impact on conversion well in excess of that 1%, you'd image that performance optimization is high on the list of priorities for theme developers, right?

Nope.

While some sites running on Shopify do take performance seriously, the vast majority of them are grossly unoptimized—they have huge images, lots of HTTP requests, and poorly structured pages.

When I started work on my own theme framework for Shopify, I conducted a "performance roundup" of existing themes in the Shopify Theme store. The results were pretty damning—the average theme in the store loaded 2MB of assets with 58 HTTP requests on page load.

I've got a theory as to why this was so: clients can't see it so they won't pay for it as a priority.

Unlike all of those pretty images or snazzy JavaScript features, a client can't "see" the speed of their sites. They might feel something's slightly amiss when a page takes ten seconds to load, but even then they're looking at their site with the mindset of a storeowner, not a potential customer. It rarely occurs to them that, had the site they were loading not been their own, they would have closed the tab five seconds ago and moved on to the next result in Google.

Designers and developers aren't immune to this problem, either. When we're sitting on a high-speed desktop connection, developing locally and with a populated browser cache, a lot of performance issues are going to go unnoticed. And just like the client, our minds aren't in the same place when the page does load—we're looking for alignment issues, checking that colors match up, and that the new lightbox works as expected.

When these factors combine, it makes it easy as a theme creator to let performance become a low priority.

This is especially true when building a theme for widespread sale (for example, in the Shopify Theme Store). There's no "sort by performance" option in the Theme Store listing—what's going to sell your theme are big glossy images and slick CSS animations.

# Performance Analysis and Metrics

So, proceeding on the assumption that you want to be one of the enlightened theme creators who takes performance seriously, what's your first move?

Well, like so many things, the first step in being able to improve performance is to know where you stand currently ("you can't manage what you can't measure" and all that). The next sections therefore look at a couple of different tools useful for doing just that.

# Performance Measuring Tools

I'll cover three tools here, but you don't need to spend too much time worrying about which one is "best". Most performance tools will cover a similar set of metrics—the key thing is to be using *something* before and after your optimization work, so that you can evaluate whether your changes had any effect.

## PageSpeed Insights

Google's PageSpeed utility is probably the most commonly-used performance analysis tool. Running the PageSpeed test from the online tool will give you a breakdown of the performance issues with your theme, as well as a prioritized list of what to tackle first (see Figure 10-1).

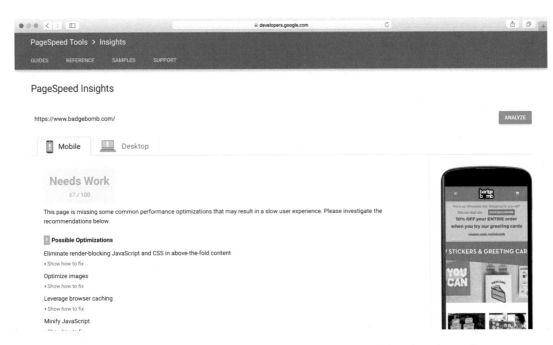

***Figure 10-1.*** *The online PageSpeed Insights tool. Looks like this theme's got some work to do!*

## Yahoo YSlow

If you have a philosophical objection to Google or just want to try something different, YSlow is a browser plugin available for both Safari and Firefox that offers much the same sort of analysis as PageSpeed (see Figure 10-2).

**Figure 10-2.** *A YSlow report in Safari*

# WebPageTest.org

This is my favorite of the various performance testing tools. Unlike the previous solution, it's not available as a browser plugin—you simply access it at `http://www.webpagetest.org` and plug in the page's URL to test.

As you can see from Figure 10-3, it's a much more advanced tool than PageSpeed or YSlow, letting you specify a huge number of variables when running the test (browser, geographic location, connection type and speed, user agent strings... the list goes on). It also lets you record the test as a video, simulate the failure of particular domains during the page load, and gives you a detailed "waterfall" timeline of your page load.

***Figure 10-3.*** *WebPageTest.org may not be the prettiest thing going around, but it provides a lot of useful detail*

A nice additional feature is the "cost analysis" of your site, indicating how much a mobile visitor may have to pay to load your site based on average mobile data rates in their country of origin. This is a nice reminder for those of us in countries where data and WiFi are plentiful.

WebPageTest.org is the only tool mentioned here that analyzes a site's *SpeedIndex*,[3] which is a way of measuring how quickly the visible parts of a page are presented to a user (often a much more important metric than the overall page load time).

## Which Tool to Use?

Unless you're itching to get into the nitty gritty of performance optimization, I recommend sticking to the simpler reports and analysis of PageSpeed Insights and YSlow for the moment. They'll identify 90% of the performance issues in your theme and indicate where you're going to see the biggest wins.

---

[3]https://sites.google.com/a/webpagetest.org/docs/using-webpagetest/metrics/speed-index.

Once you've gotten the low hanging fruit out of the way, turning to WebPageTest's detailed reports can help you identify those "one-percenters," which can often be worth spending the time on for sites with large sales volumes.

If you're looking for a way to integrate performance testing into your development workflow, check out the grunt-perfbudget Grunt plugin.[4] It's written by Tim Kadlec, who has a wealth of material on setting a "performance budget" for your site on his blog (https://timkadlec.com).

# Theme Performance Metrics

Being able to get all this performance information is great, but now the question is: how do we use it? First, it's good to have an idea of which things we should be worried about and which can be safely ignored.

In the case of Shopify themes, any performance optimizations that require server or CDN configuration are out of your hands. Fortunately, Shopify does a pretty good job of optimizing these things on their end, so we generally don't have to worry about them and can instead focus on the things that *are* under our control.

In the following sections, I've provided a list of the key metrics I look at when trying to improve my Shopify themes, along with a list of the techniques I use to try to improve those metrics. Many of these will be familiar to experienced web developers (Shopify themes are just HTML, CSS, and JavaScript at the end of the day after all), but some are Shopify-specific either in concept or execution.

The final part of this chapter focuses on each of these listed techniques in detail and walks through how to implement them.

## Key Metric 1: Page Weight

*Page weight* indicates how many bytes need to be transferred to the browser to display your site. You should be looking at two numbers here: the number of bytes transferred when the page first loads (before the browser has cached anything) and the number of bytes after caching.

Even if your site is pretty image-heavy, you should be able to deliver a usable page to a customer with a few hundred kilobytes or less. Using some of the techniques described

---

[4]https://github.com/tkadlec/grunt-perfbudget.

in this lesson, you can do this and then pull in larger assets (like high-resolution images) later as needed.

Optimization techniques that focus on reducing page weight include:

- Image optimization

- Asset minification

- Lazy loading

- Page simplification

## Key Metric 2: Number of HTTP Requests

Every HTTP request your browser makes for an asset requires a round trip from the browser to the server and back again, along with all of the overhead that implies.

Methods focused on improving the efficiency of the requests your page makes are:

- Asset concatenation

- Cookieless CDN domains (handled by Shopify)

- CDN hostname distribution (not handled by Shopify, but there's not too much we can do about it if we still want to leverage Shopify's comprehensive CDN)

- Intelligent asset loading

- Page simplification

## Key Metric 3: Time to Load

The term "time to load" is a bit imprecise, as "load" in the context of web performance can mean a few different things. It could mean:

- The time taken for the browser to load your initial HTML and start rendering the page ("time to render")

- The time taken for the browser to visually display the page to the user ("time to visual completion")

- The time taken for the entire page, including assets, to load, render, and execute ("time to load")

From the perspective of user experience, the "time to visual completion" is the most important interpretation, as it's what makes a site "feel" fast. Unfortunately, it's also the most difficult to measure with automated tools (although SpeedIndex, a metric developed by Google and thoroughly analyzed in `WebPageTest.org`'s report, does a pretty good job).

The good news is that the optimization techniques for all types of page load have some overlap, so efforts towards optimizing your initial time to render will help improve your other metrics as well. In some cases, you may wish to prioritize one type of load time over another—this is most commonly seen in techniques that attempt to get the page to an initial "visually complete" stage as fast as possible, then complete the load of additional assets.

An example of this would be the use of progressive JPEGs, which render a low-quality "first pass" image that is subsequently replaced with one of a higher quality as the page continues to load. The effect is that the user feels like the page loads much quicker, even if the overall number of bytes transferred to the user is increased, as we need to send the data for multiple versions of the image at different quality levels.

# Performance Optimization Techniques

Having identified the metrics we consider most important, we'll now get to the meat and potatoes of the chapter: identifying what you can actually do as a theme developer to improve those numbers.

# Technique 1: Page Simplification

You know the old saying, "less is more"? Well, in the case of web performance, it rings true. The "less" of your theme there is—the fewer the images, requests, and page elements—the faster your page will load and display.

Sounds sensible and straightforward, right? I agree, but it never seems to quite make it into those "Five ways to speed up your site and improve your sex life" lists on the Internet.

Perhaps the reason for its absence is that it's not always an easy, "quick win". Unlike some of the techniques we'll be looking at in a bit, taking the time to look through your hard work for things to rip out is difficult, both time-wise and emotionally. But, just like authoring good writing, authoring performant Shopify themes require ruthless editing.

The great thing about this technique is that you get some side benefits beyond the performance implications. Just like editing your writing makes things much easier for readers, editing your Shopify themes also makes things clearer and easier for your customers, as well as improving your life as a developer by reducing your maintenance burden. It's a real win-win-win!

If you're looking for ideas on the sort of things you can do to "edit down" your Shopify theme, here are some:

- *Refactor CSS*: It's easy to build up technical debt in your CSS files over the course of a site's development. Refactoring and simplifying your CSS will not only save on stylesheet size, but also make the site more maintainable and consistent for visitors.

- *Kill carousels*: Carousels are not only horrid for usability, they often load lots of high-resolution images. Do your users and your site's performance a favor by replacing the carousel with a single (optimized) image.

- *Replace background images with CSS*: CSS can do some pretty awesome stuff these days. If you're currently using tiled images for background images, consider replacing them with a CSS background. You'd be surprised at what you can do.

## Technique 2: Image Optimization

This is the first thing almost every page load optimization article will suggest. That's not a coincidence—images make up the largest percentage of the weight of most sites, and you can get some big wins with very little effort.

## Image Optimization Basics

Here's the crazy simple way to trim down your theme in less than 50 seconds:

1. Download ImageOptim from `https://imageoptim.com` and open it.

2. Drag your theme's `assets` folder into the application.

3. Wait to see how much space you just saved (see Figure 10-4).

   It really is that simple!

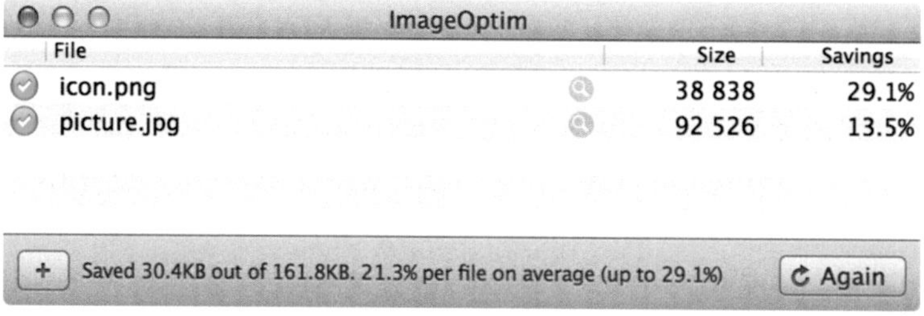

*Figure 10-4.  ImageOptim doing its thing*

As I was writing this, I ran the assets folder of a theme I've been working on through ImageOptim just to get some screenshots. I've run this theme through ImageOptim before, but I still saved 200KB of page weight from five seconds of work. Not bad!

Another tool worth checking out is JPEGMini (http://www.jpegmini.com). Unlike ImageOptim, it only handles JPEGs (who would have guessed), but it does apply some more advanced algorithms and can cut down those files even more. For those of you who aren't Mac users (sorry, I don't get out of my bubble all that often), Kraken (https://kraken.io) is a great alternative.

## Automating Image Optimization

Once you've seen the benefits of image optimization in action, you're likely going to want to use it all the time. That's when having a Grunt-based workflow like the ones described in Chapter 2 come in handy.

Using a Grunt plugin like grunt-contrib-imagemin (which is built with the same libraries used by the ImageOptim program), we can ask Grunt to automatically optimize all of our images whenever we deploy a theme. You can look back to the examples in Chapter 2 to see how this is implemented.

## Pushing Boundaries with Lossy Image Optimization

These optimization methods are "lossless"—that is, they reduce file size without any degradation in image quality. That sounds reasonable, but often we can achieve pretty spectacular reductions in file size with minor reductions in quality—some of which are going to be invisible to the end users.

Let's take JPEG images first.

If you're familiar with Photoshop's Save for Web functionality, you'll be aware that you have the option of selecting the quality of the final image. By default, this sits at

60—but the reality is that you can often drop that quality setting down to as low as 25 without ending up with a dog's breakfast. This is especially true if you're dealing with @2x or @3x images for high-resolution displays.

If you don't believe me, check out the scaling examples at `https://retinafy.me/ examples/jpeg-scaling.html` from Thomas Fuchs's excellent book *Retinafy Me*, which covers the process of creating high-resolution images in lots of helpful detail.

We can also perform lossy optimization on PNGs, thanks to a tool called ImageAlpha (developed by the same wonderful team behind ImageOptim and available at `https:// pngmini.com`).

Similar to ImageOptim, ImageAlpha enables you to drop a particular PNG file into this application, select a quality level (for PNGs, determined by the number of colors available), preview the results, and save an optimized version, as seen in Figure 10-5.

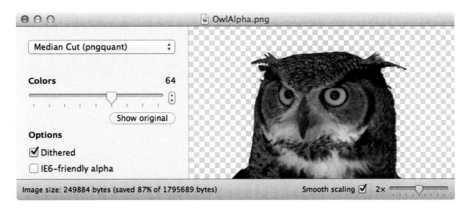

***Figure 10-5.***  *Using ImageAlpha is a hoot*

The results can be impressive, as you can see in the before/after shot in Figure 10-6.

**Figure 10-6.** *Before (above line, 224KB) and after (below, 34KB) ImageAlpha (Image courtesy of* `http://pngmini.com`*)*

Unlike lossless optimization, lossy optimization is not something I recommend automating, as you often need to run your eye over the results to make sure the optimization hasn't gone too far and verify that everything "looks right."

# Technique 3: Asset Concatenation

For every JavaScript, stylesheet, or image your page references, a client's browser needs to make an HTTP request to fetch and parse that asset. Asset concatenation is the process of combining multiple asset files into a single file to reduce the number of requests the browser must make, cutting down on this overhead and making for faster load times.

As an example, if the top of your `theme.liquid` contains something like Listing 10-1, your browser is going to be making lots of requests that it needs to wait on before it continues to render the page. A better strategy is to selectively combine these files to reduce their number, so that you end up with something more like Listing 10-2.

***Listing 10-1.*** Example theme.liquid layout File with Assets from a Variety of Sources

```
<!DOCTYPE html>
  <html>
    <head>
      <!-- Include CSS -->
      {{ 'bootstrap.css' | asset_url | stylesheet_tag }}
      {{ 'index.css' | asset_url | stylesheet_tag }}
      {{ 'products.css' | asset_url | stylesheet_tag }}
      {{ 'articles.css' | asset_url | stylesheet_tag }}

      <!-- Include Javascripts -->
      {{ 'jquery.js' | shopify_asset_url | script_tag }}
      {{ 'bootstrap-core.js' | shopify_asset_url | script_tag }}
      {{ 'bootstrap-tooltips.js' | shopify_asset_url | script_tag }}
      {{ 'bootstrap-modals.js' | shopify_asset_url | script_tag }}
      {{ 'products.js' | shopify_asset_url | script_tag }}
      {{ 'cart.js' | shopify_asset_url | script_tag }}
      ...
```

***Listing 10-2.*** Optimized Version of Listing 10-1 Utilizing Concatenated Assets

```
<!DOCTYPE html>
  <html>
    <head>
      <!-- Include CSS -->
      {{ 'main.css' | asset_url | stylesheet_tag }}

      <!-- Include Javascripts -->
      {{ 'jquery.js' | shopify_asset_url | script_tag }}
      {{ 'bootstrap.js' | shopify_asset_url | script_tag }}
      {{ 'main.js' | shopify_asset_url | script_tag }}
      ...
```

For stylesheets and JavaScript files, the concatenation is very simple—it's just a matter of copying and pasting the text contents of each file, one after another. As long as you concatenate the files in the same order that they originally appeared in your HTML, you won't notice any functional difference, but the number of requests the browser has to make is dramatically reduced.

---

**Note**  You should never include your JavaScript `<script>` tags in the `<head>` element, like in this example. Browsers will block page rendering when reading them. Put all of your tags at the bottom of your page, just before the closing `</body>` tag.

---

As with any technique, you can take this technique too far, and concatenating everything into one file can be counter-productive. In the next few sections, I've listed some things you may reasonably choose to keep separated in your themes.

## Large JavaScript Libraries

Bundling large libraries like jQuery together with your site-specific JavaScript is considered bad practice, as any changes to your site's scripts will force browsers to download everything again.

In fact, a much better strategy for large and common JavaScript libraries like jQuery is to use a common external CDN (Google's Hosted Libraries is a good start). Not only does this mean that you don't have to worry about managing the asset within your theme, there's a decent chance that site visitors will already have the library in their browser cache.

## Assets Using Theme Settings

As you saw in Chapter 8, appending a suffix to asset files (for example, `main.js.liquid`) will cause Shopify to preprocess those assets using Liquid, allowing us to use theme settings and asset filters within those files.

If your theme takes advantage of this, I recommend separating the parts of code that use the theme settings out into their own asset file as much as possible. Otherwise, you'll run in to a similar problem as that with large JavaScript libraries, forcing a large download on your users every time a theme setting changes.

If you're only using theme settings for a few minor tweaks, you could even just keep a single static asset file and add the dynamic stuff to your theme's `<head>`, as in Listing 10-3.

*Listing 10-3.* Simple Example of Using Theme Settings Inside a <style> Block

```
<!DOCTYPE html>
<html>
<head>
  <!-- Include Static CSS -->
  {{ 'main.css' | asset_url | stylesheet_tag }}

  <!-- Dynamic CSS -->
  <style>
    body {
      bgcolor: {{ settings.bgcolor | default: '#ffffff' }};
    }
  </style>

  <!-- Include Javascripts -->
  {{ 'https://ajax.googleapis.com/ajax/libs/jquery/2.1.3/jquery.min. |
script_tag }}
```

## Assets Used Only on a Specific Page

When you're bundling your assets with concatenation, the stylesheets and scripts within those files will be available across all pages on your site. This is usually a reasonable assumption to make, and even if a script isn't used on a single page, the benefits of having a single asset file usually exceed the downside of having a slightly larger file to download on some pages. However, if you have large assets that are used only on specific, rarely-used pages, it might be more efficient to keep those assets separate and load them only when needed.

A good example of this is a Shopify store that offers logged-in customers a page to view their order history and manage their account. As most visits to your site won't be from logged-in users and won't be used for account management, it makes sense to avoid bundling the scripts and styles for the account management feature together with everything else.

## Automatic Concatenation

An obvious downside to concatenation is that it makes management and development of your assets more difficult, by virtue of the fact that all of your scripts and stylesheets are now lumped together in one giant file.

Setting up a way to automatically concatenate your files means you can get the benefits of concatenation without sacrificing developer convenience. As you might have guessed, I recommend using a workflow tool to automate this process—see Chapter 2 for more.

## Image Concatenation

This section has been focused on the concatenation of scripts and stylesheets, but concatenation can be used for images as well! In fact, you've probably seen this before with CSS *sprites*, where sites use a single PNG image to hold all their icons, as shown in Figure 10-7.

*Figure 10-7.  Google's CSS sprite*

The rationale behind this is the same as with stylesheets and scripts: reducing the number of requests that need to be made improves the performance of your site.

The easiest way to do your own image concatenation is through the very excellent Grumpicon web app (http://www.grumpicon.com). It's a drag-and-drop solution that comes with the added benefit of having a unicorn involved (see Figure 10-8).

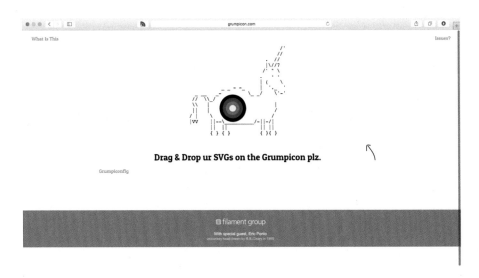

***Figure 10-8.***  *Any tool with an ASCII unicorn must be good*

Like all good asset-management tasks, the magic behind Grumpicon is available as a Grunt plugin (`grunticon`) for adding to your automated development workflow.

## Future Developments

If you've been following recent developments in web technology, you may have heard of the SPDY or HTTP2 protocols. Without getting too technical (not the least because I'm not clear on all the details myself), these are next generation technologies that aim to drastically improve the speed of the web.

One of the features of these protocols is "request multiplexing," which aims to pretty much do the equivalent of asset concatenation at a much lower level. This would mean that developers like us can just use individual assets (easier) without forcing the browser to make more requests than Madonna's rider.

However, widespread deployment and support for these protocols on servers and clients is still some time away, so for the moment you'll have to stick to the techniques as described. Sorry!

## Technique 4: Asset Minification

While stylesheets and scripts aren't usually as bulky as images, they can still have a noticeable impact on the overall weight of your pages.

Once you've followed Technique #1 and simplified and removed as much unnecessary styling and content as possible, you can use asset minification to further reduce the file size of your stylesheets and scripts.

Minification strips out the extraneous information in assets that make it easy for humans to read and write but that aren't needed by your browser (things like newlines and whitespace). In the case of JavaScript, minification can also aggressively optimize your code size by doing things like rewriting `var aLongVariableNameUsefulForHumans` to `var a`.

## How to Minify Your Assets

If you want to experiment with minification or just want to perform a one-off minification, there are plenty of online tools that will take a CSS or JavaScript file and spit out the minified version (just Google "CSS/JavaScript minifier"). However, minification is at its most useful when we can slot it into the workflow once and not have to think about it again. Once again, the Grunt plugins `grunt-contrib-cssmin` and `grunt-contrib-uglify` come to your rescue with CSS and JavaScript minification, respectively.

If you have a different workflow process or would like to perform minification from the command line, you can check out the comprehensive *YUICompressor*, which handles both CSS and JavaScript. The *uglify* tool is also available as a standalone JavaScript minifier that can be run from the command line.

# Technique 5: Odds and Ends

Properly implementing all these techniques will, in most cases, get you a long way toward improving your theme's performance. If, like me, you're a little bit obsessive about performance or are in a situation where extracting every last ounce/gram of speed is going to materially affect a store's bottom line, there are still a couple more things you can do.

## Implement Device-Responsive Design

Before "responsive design" came to mean that thing we do by dragging the width of our browser back and forth, it had a broader meaning—that web sites could respond to a whole range of contexts to deliver the best experience.

A good example of where this idea comes in handy in the performance arena is with "retina" or "high-resolution" images. A common technique for high-resolution images over the last few years has been to simply serve all clients a high-res image resized to be half the size. Browsers then do the work of resizing and displaying appropriately.

The problem with this approach is that it's very wasteful when serving to screens that aren't high-resolution—they're downloading an image that is four times the size for no advantage. "Device-responsive design" takes this sort of thing into account by only loading high-resolution images on high-resolution devices, either using media queries or a JavaScript library.

## Use Lazy Loading

This technique can be really powerful for Shopify stores, as they are often very image-heavy. Lazy loading images involves using a JavaScript library to only load images when they should be visible in the user's viewport, improving initial page load times.

It's especially handy when your theme involves very tall pages where lots of visitors won't actually need to load the majority of your content. Matt Mlinac's lazy load jQuery plugin (`http://www.appelsiini.net/projects/lazyload`) is a very solid implementation.

## Use Conditional Loading for Shims/Fallbacks

If you're using "shims" or fallbacks for older browsers (for example, the RespondJS fallback that allows older browsers like Internet Explorer 8 to use media queries), make sure you're not wastefully downloading them on newer browsers.

You can implement this by using conditional comments when loading the script, as in Listing 10-4, or by using JavaScript-based conditional loading based on the results of testing with a library like Modernizr.

***Listing 10-4.*** Using Conditional Comments to Load a Respond.js Fallback on Internet Explorer 8 and Lower

```
<!DOCTYPE html>
<html lang="en" prefix="og: http://ogp.me/ns#">
<head>
    <!-- HTML5 shim and Respond.js support for HTML5 elements and media
    queries -->
```

```
<!--[if lt IE 9]>
  <script src="{{ 'js-html5shiv-min.js' | asset_url }}"></script>
  <script src="{{ 'js-respond-min.js' | asset_url }}"></script>
<![endif]-->
...
```

## Master the "async" Attribute

As mentioned, putting `<script>` tags in the `<head>` section of your HTML is a sure-fire way to kill your page loading times, as browsers will block page rendering while they wait for your JavaScript to load. Common wisdom says that the best place for including `script` tags on your page is at the very bottom of the page, just before the `</body>` tag.

This is a great default approach, but with the advent of HTML5, we now have access to the `async` attribute for script elements, which tells browsers to continue parsing and rendering the page while loading the script in the background.

However, there are some major caveats to the use of `async`—namely, that there are no guarantees on execution time or order. If you're interested in diving into the nuts and bolts of `async`, Jake Archibald's walkthrough at `http://www.html5rocks.com/en/tutorials/speed/script-loading/` is the best I've read.

## Check for Asset 404s and 301s

Look through the Network panel or similar in your browser's developer tools and check that no assets are 404-ing or 301-ing.

Missing assets (404s) are a waste of a request and you should just remove the reference to the asset or replace it with one that works—this problem can be compounded if the site itself has a large or complex custom 404 page that needs to be downloaded any time an asset is missing.

An asset request being redirected with a 301 response code is actually quite common (for example, a request to an `http://` version of an asset may be automatically redirected to the `https://` version). If you see that happening, just link directly to the final URL to avoid the wasted initial request.

# Evaluating Performance Improvements

Once you've made each performance optimization, it's always a good idea to measure your performance metrics again to see what's changed. Not only will this give you a sense of achievement and motivate you, you'll start to get a good idea of where the easy optimizations are and start to incorporate them into your normal development workflow.

Now, while all this measuring is handy, there's nothing quite like actually using your site to check whether your customers are getting a good experience! Next time you're on a train, or out with your phone in an area with patchy reception, try clearing your browser cache and loading your site. Bonus points for asking random strangers in coffee shops to do the same and try to buy something from your store.

If you can't wait to get out of the home or office to test your performance improvements and you have a Mac, you can use OS X's Network Link Conditioner, seen in Figure 10-9. Turn your connection settings down to spotty 2G and see if your site holds up.

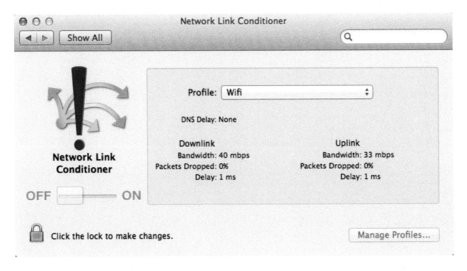

***Figure 10-9.*** *Condition that link!*

Get instructions on how to set up the network link conditioner at `http://nshipster.com/network-link-conditioner/`.

Chrome users (both on Mac and Windows) have access to a similar feature (called Throttling) in the Network tab of Developer Tools.

# Final Thoughts

Performance optimization is one of those tasks that pays significant dividends for storeowners, but still gets overlooked during development and testing, as it's very easy to subconsciously paper over a site's issues.

Remember: as a theme developer, you *have* to wait for a Shopify store to load (it's your job). Customers don't have that obligation, and they will leave in favor of a competitor at the drop of a hat.

# Summary

This chapter explored why performance is simultaneously one of the most important yet most often overlooked aspects of theme development. The chapter dug in to the motivation for improving theme performance and discussed the key metrics to track along with the tools to track them.

With an understanding of what you were trying to improve under your belt, you learned about a number of specific strategies and techniques you can use to ensure your themes load quickly and provide a responsive customer experience.

# CHAPTER 11

# Collaborative Theme Development

This final chapter looks at some strategies and tools you can use to make it easier to build Shopify themes in collaboration with others. It will also discuss how you can deploy your themes in a professional manner to reduce the risk of downtime, conflicts, or errors on the theme being used by your customers.

Finally, I'll wrap up the substantive part of this book by discussing how you can make the most of Shopify's ecosystem to boost your understanding of the platform and forge deeper connections within the partner community.

## Collaborating on Themes

The previous chapters covered the core components of Shopify themes, discussed different approaches to building them, and walked through the development of an example theme. These discussions have been working on two assumptions—that we're working in a team size of one, and that our code is being uploaded directly to the Shopify site it's being used on.

In the real world, this often isn't the case—themes can be built by teams of many developers, designers, and content editors. Furthermore, when your themes are being used "in production" by merchants, having a professional deployment process becomes important to reduce the risk of errors being introduced to a store and potentially causing revenue loss.

Even if you're a solo developer and don't anticipate that changing, following the practices we're about to outline will not only make your single-person workflow smoother, it'll also mean that developers taking over a project (or yourself coming back to a theme after a couple of months' break) get the benefit of a smooth, clearly defined workflow.

© Gavin Ballard 2017
G. Ballard, *The Definitive Guide to Shopify Themes*, DOI 10.1007/978-1-4842-2641-4_11

# Collaborative Workflows with Version Control

Recall Chapter 2, which discussed how to place your theme files under version control with Git—a vital first step if you plan on working on themes with other people. To recap:

- Version control provides a way to track changes to your theme files, and provides an easy way to recover from accidentally overwritten or deleted files.

- It provides a way to record who was responsible for specific changes to a theme and allows multiple developers to work on a project at the same time before "merging" changes.

- You can use feature branches and multiple preview themes to develop new code and theme features independently of the live theme.

To turn this into a modern collaborative development workflow, we only need to add a couple of things to the mix:

- A centralized server (or a decentralized process) allowing multiple developers to push their own changes and fetch the changes of others.

- A system for organizing what needs to be done and who needs to be doing it.

- A process for reviewing changes before they are merged into the main codebase.

There are about as many different workflows for this sort of thing as there are developers, so I won't attempt a comprehensive list. Instead, here's a description of the typical workflow we use at my company for managing this process (we use GitHub as a central code repository, for listing and tracking issues, and for reviewing and merging changes):

- A new code repository is created on GitHub, and the relevant team members are given access to the code. If we're building a theme from scratch, someone will create the initial set of files locally using Slate or our own theme framework. If we're working with an existing theme, we'll use Slate, Theme Kit, or Shopify's .zip export feature to fetch the current set of files and commit them to the repository as a starting point.

- Each team member creates their own unpublished "preview theme" on the store we're working on, to ensure that any changes they make don't affect the live site or other developers, but can still make use of "real" store data.

- We identify the work to be done and break it into small, discrete features that are added as "Issues" in GitHub. Work is divvied up by assigning those issues to individual team members.

- When tackling a new issue, a developer will create a new "feature branch" specific to that issue and work on it with their code changes automatically updating the personal preview theme.

- Once happy with the changes, the developer will create a GitHub pull request asking to merge the changes into the "master" branch of the repository. Another team member (usually the project's technical lead) is assigned to review the changes (see Figure 11-1). Once feedback is given and any required changes are made, the changes are merged into the "master" branch of the repository and the process repeats with the next issue.

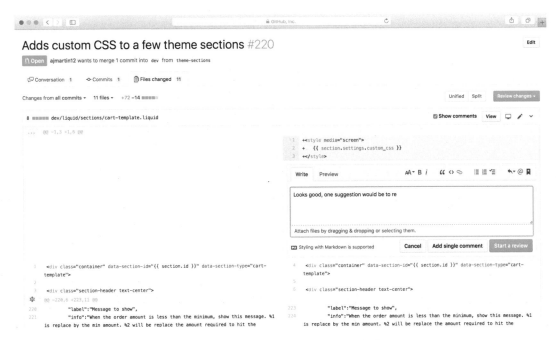

***Figure 11-1.*** *A theme code review in progress on GitHub*

Using a process like this and only deploying the "master" branch to the published theme on a Shopify store ensures that developers aren't accidentally overwriting or duplicating each other's work. When using code review before merging changes into the "master" branch, it also ensures all changes get a second pair of eyes on them.

# Collaborative Deployment Processes

Once we have a system in place for assigning tasks, working on them independently, and then reviewing and merging changes, the next question is how can we roll out that consolidated version of the theme. Before discussing that, let's review the processes you've learned about so far.

Early in Chapter 2, when you saw how to move theme development to a local machine, the deployment workflow looked like something in Figure 11-2. Changes made locally were being uploaded directly to the Shopify store's published theme via Theme Kit or Slate.

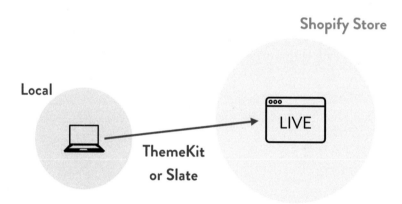

***Figure 11-2.*** *The early deployment workflow, with changes being uploaded directly to the published theme*

As also discussed in Chapter 2, this sort of workflow has some issues:

- Having changes made locally uploaded instantly into production makes it easy to introduce errors that affect real customers. There's no quality control mechanism like testing or code review between the developer and the production code.

- If multiple developers are working on a theme, it's easy to accidentally overwrite each other's changes but difficult to roll back to a known point in time.

- It becomes difficult or impossible to know what state the live theme is in.

Figure 11-3 describes an improvement over this. Here, the Shopify store has multiple themes in play—a "development" theme (if you have multiple people working on the theme, then you'll likely have at least one theme per developer) and a "live" theme. It still uses Theme Kit or Slate to automatically upload changes to the development theme as we make them locally, but because this theme isn't published, the real-time changes won't affect real customers.

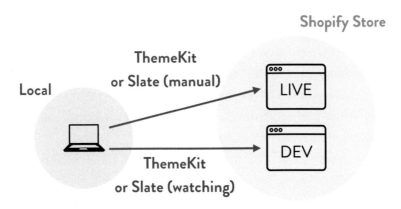

***Figure 11-3.*** *A slightly improved deployment workflow, with separate development and live themes*

Using this workflow, once a developer is happy with the state of the development theme (and they have pulled in any changes from other developers), the developer can "deploy" the final theme state by pointing Theme Kit or Slate at the live version of the theme and running a full upload from the command line with theme replace.

This improvement avoids the biggest problem—accidentally making a change that ends up affecting customers—but we still run the risk of overwriting other's code, have no proper QA process, and can't tell what state a theme is in.

We can improve this further by adding an intermediate step between the code on our local development machine and the production version of our theme—a central repository—as shown in Figure 11-4.

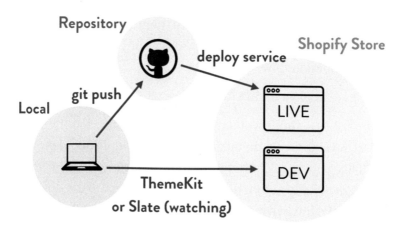

***Figure 11-4.*** *Adding a code repository between the local development machine and the production version of the code*

By adding this step, we enforce a rule that only code from the central repository and on a specific version control branch ("master" or perhaps "production") can be deployed to the live theme. This ensures that all changes go through a quality assurance process, such as code review and perhaps some automated testing, before being merged to the main branch and rolled out into production.

To facilitate the deployment of your theme code out to the live theme, it's necessary to use some form of deployment service. Your options here will vary, depending on the service you're using to host your repository and what integrations are available. A common choice in the Shopify world (and the choice I'm most familiar with) is DeployBot (see `https://deploybot.com`). DeployBot, shown in Figure 11-5, has native support for connecting to a specific Shopify theme and deploying code to it from a variety of version control sources (such as GitHub).

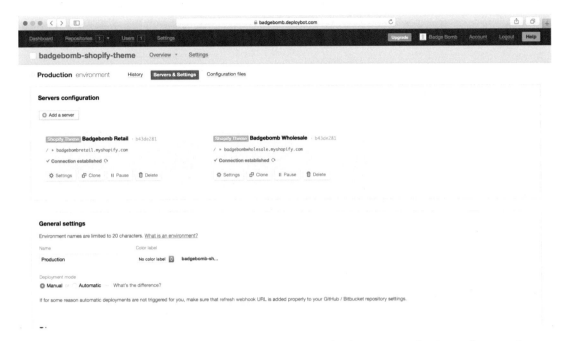

***Figure 11-5.*** *A DeployBot configuration screen linking a single GitHub repository to two production versions of a Shopify theme (one for retail and one for wholesale)*

Deployment services like DeployBot can be configured to deploy your theme code to a Shopify store either manually (triggered by logging in and clicking a button), or automatically (triggered by simply pushing or merging code to a specific branch of your theme repository).

The process you choose may vary from project to project, but I commonly set up two deployment triggers—one to automatically deploy all changes to the "master" branch of a repository to a "staging" version of the theme, and then one that must be triggered manually to roll out the final changes to the production store (see Figure 11-6).

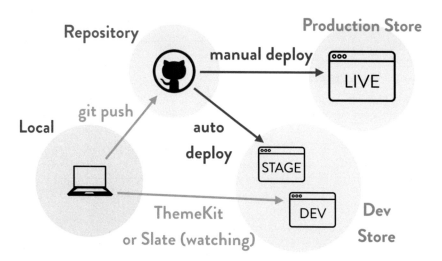

***Figure 11-6.*** *A production-ready deployment workflow, including automated and manual deployment triggers and multiple Shopify stores*

As you'll see, Figure 11-6 also shows the separation of the live theme from the staging and development themes by placing them on separate Shopify stores. This is often a good practice to further reduce the risks of your development workflow accidentally affecting real customers, as well as allowing you to separate test data (such as orders, products, and customers) from "production" data.

In some real-world scenarios, your workflow may be even more complex, with many more Shopify stores, each containing live or staging themes. This may occur when you're using a single codebase to drive many different "variants" of a Shopify store (for example, retail/wholesale variants for a single brand, or variants targeted at different locales). In situations like this, having an automated deploy service becomes essential to avoid inconsistent theme states and to properly manage your development processes.

## Cloning Shopify Stores

Some of the more "advanced" deployment scenarios I mentioned involve creating one or more "development" Shopify stores to allow for experimentation without affecting live store data. Generally, it's a good idea to keep the product, collection, page, and theme data on your production stores as up to date with the real store as possible, so that you're developing in a more "realistic" environment.

Shopify does enable you to export and import product and theme data (although keeping your theme up to date should be the responsibility of developers and your deployment service), but unfortunately there's no built-in way to automate this or to import/export other data like page, collection, and blog content.

Aside from a periodic manual synchronization process, there are a couple of options. The first is to install one of the many "store sync" applications available in the Shopify App store. Depending on the type and quantity of data you need to synchronize, using one or more of these apps can be an easy way to keep your development stores up to date.

The second option (and my own preferred method) is to use the freely available Quickshot tool (see `https://quickshot.readme.io`). While this tool was originally built to synchronize theme data from a local machine to a Shopify store (similar to the functionality now provided by Slate, discussed in Chapter 2), it also contains tools to synchronize product, collection, blog, and page data.

# The Shopify Theme Store

I'd imagine that many readers have picked up this book with one eye toward the Shopify theme store (see `https://themes.shopify.com`). From the store, shown in Figure 11-7, merchants can purchase new themes to use on their stores. The rewards of getting your theme listed on the theme store can be significant; while Shopify doesn't publish the official numbers, it's estimated that a top ten theme on the store earns between $15,000 and $25,000 per month in sales, with the top ten theme authors (many of whom have multiple themes listed) earn between $25,000 to $50,000 per month.

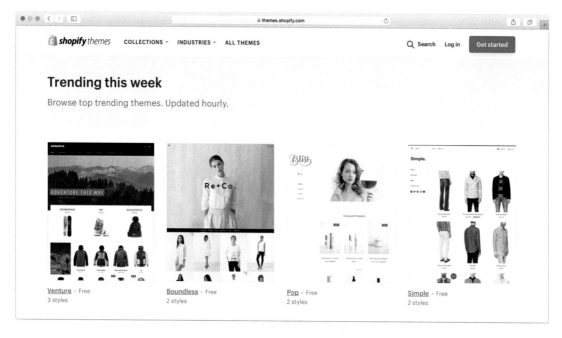

*Figure 11-7.* *The Shopify theme store*

These numbers are supported by Shopify maintaining "premium" pricing for themes (between $140 and $180 per install) and having a very, very strict submissions process that keeps the number of themes limited (only 55 themes are available at the time of writing, with each theme containing 2-4 preset styles). While this process means that only a small percentage of submissions make it to be published, the rest of this section looks at what you can do to maximize your chances, as well as covers some fallback options to consider in the event that your submission is rejected.

# Getting In to the Theme Store

Obviously, there's no magical trick to getting in to the theme store. You need to have experience with theme design and development, a solid concept, and the willingness to put in a lot of hard work—in the design, revision, and submission phases, and also once you launch your theme. It's unlikely that the first theme you develop or submit will make it through the review process.

That said, there are always some things you can do to maximize your chances of success.

# Familiarize Yourself with the Process

According to the Shopify Themes Team, the number one mistake they see theme developers make is rushing head-first into development and spending a lot of time and effort on a theme build, only to have it rejected at step one because it doesn't address a need on the store or is too similar to an existing theme.

Shopify has a detailed explanation of their process available at `https://themes.shopify.com/services/themes/guidelines`, which outlines three key steps. These are:

- The submission of a theme brief, covering the vision of the theme, a description of the unmet merchant needs addressed by your theme, and details about how your theme will be implemented and the team behind it.

- The submission of interactive mobile design prototypes using Invision or a similar tool.

- The submission of interactive desktop design prototypes using Invision or a similar tool.

You should get detailed feedback from the Shopify Themes Team at each step before spending your time moving to the next stage. The first hurdle is probably the hardest to get past—your theme brief needs to make a convincing case for why your theme will address a real-world problem merchants have, without becoming too niche or vertical-specific.

Approval of your theme brief by Shopify doesn't automatically guarantee final entry to the theme store, but if your brief is sufficiently detailed and your final product addresses the brief completely, you'll have the best possible chance.

# Have a Novel or Unique Angle

The Shopify Themes Team states:

> What we need to see is a project brief that consists of both subjective opinions and objective research, that outlines the necessity and validity of a perceived problem, opportunity, and solution.

When evaluating that perceived problem and solution, you'll need to keep clear of broad and subjective statements ("there aren't enough themes that make good use of flat design") or just providing a list of features your theme will offer ("multi-level navigation menus, image carousels, and slick quick shop functionality"). Instead, start thinking at a higher level about the types of merchants you think might be your customers, and why your theme will help them where existing themes don't. ("Merchants who focus on selling a select range of digital products are underserved as most themes focus on merchants selling physical goods. My theme will address this by offering merchants useful functionality that only makes sense in a digital context and can help increase conversions for those types of products.")

## Work Closely with the Themes Team

While the Themes Team will always be willing to provide feedback and advice on your theme's brief and prototypes as you move through the submission process, it's important to pay close attention to the feedback you are getting from them and revise your submission to address any of their concerns.

You don't have an unlimited number of revisions to play with before your submission will be permanently rejected, so try to gather as much detail as possible about any concerns held by the Themes Team. If something in their feedback isn't clear, ask for clarification—even better, provide your reviewer a few alternatives to an original suggestion to reduce their workload and come up with something they can get behind.

## Follow the Theme Liquid and Content Guidelines

To ensure you know what you're getting yourself into, make sure you read the Themes Team's Liquid requirements (`https://help.shopify.com/themes/development/theme-store-requirements/theme-file-requirements`) and content checklist (`https://help.shopify.com/themes/development/theme-store-requirements/content-style-guide`) before starting the submission process.

The number of things checked by the Themes Team with respect to functionality, accessibility, and content often catches developers off guard when it comes to planning their development timelines.

## Be Ready for Support

Shopify offers two revenue split models for theme developers: 70/30 and 50/50. The 70/30 split is offered where the developer agrees to handle support for the theme, while under the 50/50 model, Shopify fields inbound support.

It's important to note, however, that the 50/50 split is only offered on a case-by-case basis, so even if you're thinking of forgoing the extra 20% revenue, you should be prepared to handle a significant number of support requests. Anecdotally, I think Shopify will rarely be offering the 50/50 model to theme developers moving forward, due to the resource demands and difficulties of supporting a third-party product.

Providing a clear plan for how you and your team (if you have one) will provide quality, dedicated customer support is an essential component of your theme briefing document, as it assures Shopify they won't end up fielding complaints about unresponsive theme developers.

# What to Do if Your Theme Doesn't Make It

No matter how much time and effort you spend on submitting a theme to the theme store, the numbers say there's a high likelihood of rejection. While that can be disheartening (I should know, the first few designs I helped submit to the Themes Team were rejected), all isn't lost. There are still ways that you can extract value from your hard work.

## Go It Alone

The first approach I recommend is to simply set up your own landing page offering the theme for sale (you can and should do this even if you're accepted into the theme store, by the way). Write your landing page content to target storeowners that have a specific use case that your theme can show off, but isn't found in the regular theme store.

The advantage of this approach is that your cut of the proceeds is 100% minus processing costs, rather than 70%. The downside, obviously, is that it's going to be much more difficult to drive sales outside of the official channel, and the price point for such themes tends to be lower (in the $50 to $100 range).

In recent times, established Shopify theme developers have experimented with selling themes at a *higher* price point outside the Shopify theme store. One perfect example of this is the "Turbo" theme in Figure 11-8 from long-term developers Out of the Sandbox, which currently retails at $350. While this has been a successful strategy for them, and has more fairly compensated them for the time required to support their themes, I imagine it would be difficult for a non-established developer with no existing customer base to follow this approach.

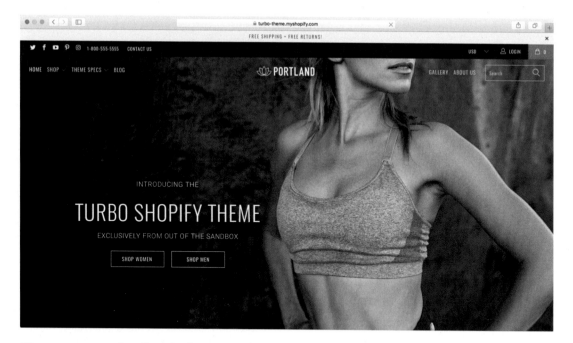

*Figure 11-8.   This "Turbo" theme is sold outside the theme store by Out of the Sandbox*

## Use Alternative Theme Marketplaces

Sites like ThemeForest (`https://themeforest.net`) and Creative Market (`https://creativemarket.com`) offer alternative theme marketplaces for you to list your theme. These sites tend to be a race to the bottom with price, so expect to be selling your themes for $30-$50 here. The quality of themes on offer is often (but not always) quite low.

## Framework-ize

Most Shopify theme developers building bespoke themes for clients eventually start to develop their own "framework" for themes—a set of starting templates and styles to avoid going through the same steps again and again. Consider extracting parts of what you've built into your own framework or pattern library to get a head start the next time you work on a project for a client.

## Use Open-Source

You won't make any money directly from this strategy, but open-sourcing your theme can be a great way to get yourself in front of more savvy clients and other theme developers. This in turn can generate inbound leads for custom development work. The next section discusses some of the benefits of open-sourcing your Shopify work.

# Leveraging the Shopify Ecosystem

When I started working as a Shopify Expert, I didn't have that much interaction with other developers. I was comfortable just doing my own thing, and I managed to get by with the clients I had coming in through the experts listing or word of mouth referrals.

After a couple of years tinkering around with the platform, I built up the confidence to start publishing the occasional article on my personal blog. It wasn't anything game-changing—mostly just describing how I was working around some of Shopify's limitations at the time, like getting the Respond.js library to work on Shopify's CDN.[1] I got some positive feedback from other developers (both in and outside Shopify), so I continued putting out the occasional Shopify-related post.

Over time, knowing that my blog content was being read and found useful gave me the courage to start putting other things I was working on out into the wild. Since then, I've released a paid framework to help people build themes using the Bootstrap frontend framework, developed a bunch of open-source projects to aid with Shopify development (visible at https://github.com/discolabs), recorded several screencasts on theme and app development, delivered talks and workshops about Shopify at meetups and conferences around the world, and now have written this book.

None of these projects led the way to untold riches, or spun up into a hugely popular and closely followed project (although one, Cart.js, was used by Kanye West's Yeezy store, which was pretty cool). Despite not reaping huge financial reward directly, in every case I feel like I've gotten something back:

- I've gotten lots of warm and fuzzies when complete strangers said nice things about my articles or projects.

- I've gotten even more warm and fuzzies when complete strangers paid for my articles or projects.

---

[1]http://gavinballard.com/using-respond.js-with-shopify/

- The number of inquiries from higher-quality clients has increased, and selling clients becomes easier when one can say they've literally written the book on Shopify.

- My relationship with one of my very best clients, which started years ago with them asking me to make a single tweak to my paid framework, is still ongoing and profitable (for both of us!)

- I've been able to connect with and meet some really great folks in the Shopify ecosystem.

The point of going through all this isn't meant to be the world's longest humble brag, but more to highlight that sharing your work with the community, however small the contribution, can lead to lots of interesting opportunities and pay real dividends.

Now that you're reaching the end of this book, you're hopefully in a position where you feel more confident about tackling your next Shopify theme development project. (Well, I certainly hope you are—if not, you'd better get in touch with me to let me know what needs to improve for the next edition.)

As you work on that project, I encourage you to think about how the things you're learning and developing could be turned into something valuable for the wider community. When I say "community," I'm not referring to anything official. There's no admission process or secret handshake. I also don't believe that you need to have years and years of experience with Shopify to teach others something valuable.

It might be a blog post describing how you overcame a difficulty when building your theme, or replying to someone who's asked a question on the Shopify forums. Even just raising an issue on GitHub for an open-source library you've been using is super useful and will be very much appreciated by the maintainers!

A rising tide lifts all boats, and having a Shopify developer community that's vibrant and full of active and supportive members is only going to encourage the ecosystem's growth.

# Where to Join

This section contains a list of resources that I think are useful for participating in the Shopify community.

# Official Shopify Channels

Shopify has a number of "official" channels for communicating with developers and partners and facilitating community discussion. The key ones are:

- The Shopify Forums (`https://ecommerce.shopify.com/forums`) are great place to start searching when looking for answers to questions you might have about Shopify concepts or development. One of the best ways to build up a reputation in the community is by helping other people out here, or posting about your own experiences.

- Make sure you're subscribed to Shopify's various blogs via RSS or e-mail. There are three official blogs—one targeted at merchants (`https://www.shopify.com/blog`), one at partners and developers (`https://www.shopify.com/partners/blog`), and one focused on the enterprise offering Shopify Plus (`https://www.shopify.com/enterprise`). Figure 11-9 shows the partner blog.

- Two "official" Shopify podcasts currently exist—the infrequently-updated but in-depth Shopify Partners Podcast, hosted by Keir Whitaker (`https://soundcloud.com/shopify-partners`) and the merchant-focused Shopify Masters Podcast (`https://www.shopify.com/blog/topics/podcasts`), hosted by Felix Thea.

- There's an official Shopify Partners Slack community, which is open to all registered Shopify partners. Once you're registered, introduce yourself to your Partner Manager and ask for an invite.

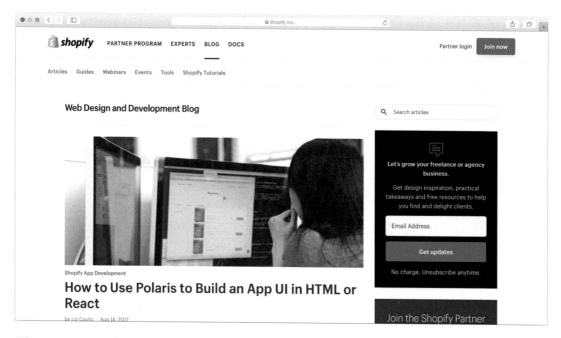

**Figure 11-9.**   *The Shopify Partner blog contains a constant stream of information for developers and partners interested in Shopify*

## Other Resources

Of course, one of the things that makes Shopify great is the multitude of community-driven groups and initiatives. Some of the stand-outs to take note of are:

- The Unofficial Shopify Podcast, hosted by Kurt Elster (`http://www.unofficialshopifypodcast.com`). It's merchant-focused but often contains plenty of useful, actionable advice for developers and other partners who'd like to learn skills that can benefit storeowners.

- The eCommTalk Slack channel, run by TJ Mapes (`http://ecommtalk.com`). A great mix of partners, marketers and merchants, this community contains plenty of experienced people willing to help out fellow Shopify developers.

- The Shopify Entrepreneurs Facebook group, run by Jonathan Kennedy (`https://www.facebook.com/groups/shopifyentrepreneurs/`). Not that technically-minded, but it's a great way to connect with and help out aspiring Shopify merchants, so for a developer it's fertile ground for honing theme development skills.

# IRL Events

If you're itching to meet up with others in the Shopify community offline, there are plenty of opportunities to do that as well. In 2016, Shopify starting supporting a network of "official" Shopify Meetups around the globe, a network that's been expanding at an increasing pace. You can find a list of upcoming meetups on the Partner Events page on the Shopify site (`https://www.shopify.com/partners/blog/partner-events`).

There's also Unite, Shopify's annual partner conference and where the company makes major feature announcements. In addition, Shopify often supports or runs local workshops and satellite one-day conferences around the globe. Contact your Partner Manager at Shopify to find out what's coming up in your corner of the world.

# Use Open-Source

Finally, one of the best resources to leverage when working on Shopify projects is GitHub (yes, other open-source platforms are available). Not only does Shopify tend to release a lot of their code as "official" open-source repositories, but third-party developers and experts from around the world have shared their own projects, tools, and code snippets as well.

Apart from releasing several of our own open-source projects, my company has also used (and later contributed to) existing libraries like the Ruby and Python Shopify API clients or the Shopify App gem. Fixing problems you run into and contributing your patches back into a project helps everyone and can often lead to opportunities to work with interesting clients.

Being familiar with the open-source process can also be an advantage when trying to resolve issues on behalf of clients. In some cases, you're able to have a direct conversation with the developers trying to resolve a bug in the Shopify codebase.[2]

# Summary

To wrap up this chapter (and the substantive portion of this book), I want to emphasize how much I see the collaborative nature of Shopify's partner ecosystem as key to the platform's success. In my years working on the platform, I have almost without exception

---

[2]As an example, check out `https://github.com/Shopify/active_shipping/pull/170#issuecomment-50399499`, where I was able to work directly with the Shopify developers responsible for the shipping logic to resolve a problem for a client of ours.

been greeted with warmth, patience, and helpfulness from others in the Shopify community as I've reached out with questions or requests.

Simply pinging a fellow expert on Twitter or dropping someone a line via e-mail has led to fruitful discussions, interesting client work, and the occasional friendship, as it turns out that most people are happy to discuss their work and share what they know.

Take @gavinballard on Twitter as an example—he's always keen to chat Shopify and greet new followers!

# Index

© Gavin Ballard 2017
G. Ballard, *The Definitive Guide to Shopify Themes*, DOI 10.1007/978-1-4842-2641-4

# Get the eBook for only $5!

Why limit yourself?

With most of our titles available in both PDF and ePUB format, you can access your content wherever and however you wish—on your PC, phone, tablet, or reader.

Since you've purchased this print book, we are happy to offer you the eBook for just $5.

To learn more, go to http://www.apress.com/companion or contact support@apress.com.

# Apress®

Printed in the United States
By Bookmasters